KU-648-612

TO. OUR. FRIENDS. OF.
THE. SHAKESPEARE.BIRTHPLACE.TRUST.
AND.
THE. SHAKESPEARE.INSTITUTE.
ALL. HAPPINESS.
AND. THAT. ETERNITY.
PROMISED.
BY.
OUR. EVER-LIVING.POET.
WISH.
THE. WELL-WISHING.
ADVENTURERS.IN.SETTING.
FORTH. THESE.ENSUING. CHAPTERS.

PME·SWW

Acknowledgements

We should like to record our gratitude to: Dr James Binns, for information relating to the Greek Anthology and to Prudentius; Professor Julia Briggs; Signor Lucca Carpaccio, for assistance with Italian sources; Alec Cobbe; David Crane; Professor Katherine Duncan-Jones, for the kind loan of an unpublished paper on theatrical adaptations of the Sonnets and for information on Thomas Thorpe; Dr Lorna Flint, for assistance with rhyme schemes in Shakespeare's plays; Rachel Gatiss; Professor Christa Jahnson; MacDonald P. Jackson; Professor Russell Jackson; Dr Paul Prescott; Andrew Rawle, for the loan of videos; Dr Peter J. Smith; William Sutton; Judith Wardman; and the librarians of the Shakespeare Centre and the Shakespeare Institute, Stratford-upon-Avon, for many courtesies. Professor Peter Holland, as joint General Editor of the series, has made many invaluable suggestions.

Readers may welcome a note about the method of collaboration undertaken by the authors. Paul Edmondson suggested the idea and, after preliminary talks, each author independently drafted a proposal. These were refined following further discussion between the authors and in the light of comments received from Peter Holland (as joint General Editor of the series) and from readers appointed by the Press. The final proposal indicated which of the authors would be primarily responsible for which chapter, and in some cases that authorship of single chapters would be shared. As writing proceeded, each author scrutinized what the other had written, and revised his work in the light of subsequent discussion. Each author read successive drafts, and again revisions were discussed and agreed. We believe the final work to be the result of an equal and happy collaboration in which neither of us felt any need to compromise his own opinions in favour of the other's.

Chapter 2, 'The History and Emergence of the Sonnet as a Literary Form', draws upon chapter 2, 'The Originality of Shakespeare's Sonnets', in Stanley Wells's *Looking for Sex in Shakespeare* (Cambridge: Cambridge University Press, 2004).

PME; SW

Oxford Shakespeare Topics

Shakespeare's Sonnets

OXFORD SHAKESPEARE TOPICS

Published and forthcoming titles include:

Oxford Shakespeare Topics

GENERAL EDITORS: PETER HOLLAND AND STANLEY WELLS

Shakespeare's Sonnets

PAUL EDMONDSON AND STANLEY WELLS

OXFORD

UNIVERSITY PRESS

OXFORD
UNIVERSITY PRESS

Great Clarendon Street, Oxford OX2 6DP

Oxford University Press is a department of the University of Oxford.
It furthers the University's objective of excellence in research, scholarship, and education by publishing worldwide in

Oxford New York

Auckland Cape Town Dar es Salaam Hong Kong Karachi
Kuala Lumpur Madrid Melbourne Mexico City Nairobi
New Delhi Shanghai Taipei Toronto

With offices in

Argentina Austria Brazil Chile Czech Republic France Greece
Guatemala Hungary Italy Japan South Korea Poland Portugal
Singapore Switzerland Thailand Turkey Ukraine Vietnam

Oxford is a registered trade mark of Oxford University Press
in the UK and in certain other countries

Published in the United States
by Oxford University Press Inc., New York

British Library Cataloguing in Publication Data
Data available
Library of Congress Cataloging in Publication Data
Data available

ISBN 0-19-925610-1
ISBN 0-19-925611-x (pbk.)

3 5 7 9 10 8 6 4 2

Typeset by Kolam Information Services Pvt. Ltd, Pondicherry, India
Printed in Great Britain
on acid-free paper by
Antony Rowe Ltd.,
Chippenham, Wiltshire

Contents

List of Illustrations

Barnfield	Richard Barnfield, *The Complete Poems*, ed. George Klawitter (Selinsgrove: Susquehanna University Press, 1990)
Booth, *Essay*	Stephen Booth, *An Essay on Shakespeare's Sonnets* (New Haven: Yale University Press, 1969)
Booth, *Sonnets*	*Shakespeare's Sonnets*, edited with analytical commentary by Stephen Booth (New Haven: Yale University Press, 1977)
Burrow	*The Complete Sonnets and Poems*, ed. Colin Burrow, The Oxford Shakespeare (Oxford: Oxford University Press, 2002; repr. with corrections, 2003)
Duncan-Jones	*Shakespeare's Sonnets*, ed. Katherine Duncan-Jones, The Arden Shakespeare, 3rd ser. (London: Thomas Nelson, 1997)
Hammond, *Figuring Sex*	Paul Hammond, *Figuring Sex between Men from Shakespeare to Rochester* (Oxford: Clarendon Press, 2002)
Hammond, *Love between Men*	Paul Hammond, *Love between Men in English Literature* (Basingstoke: Macmillan, 1996)
Kerrigan	*The Sonnets and 'A Lover's Complaint'*, ed. John Kerrigan, New Penguin Shakespeare (Harmondsworth: Penguin Books, 1986)
Lee	*Elizabethan Sonnets*, Arber's English Garner, ed. with introd. by Sidney Lee, 2 vols. (London, 1904; repr. New York: Cooper Square Publishers Inc., 1964)
Malone	Edmond Malone, *Supplement to the Edition of Shakespeare's Plays published in 1778* (1780)
Rollins	*The Sonnets*, ed. Hyder E. Rollins, New Variorum Shakespeare, 2 vols. (Philadelphia: Lippincott, 1944)

Spiller	Michael G. Spiller, *The Development of the Sonnet* (London: Routledge, 1992)
Vendler	Helen Vendler (ed.), *The Art of Shakespeare's Sonnets* (Cambridge, Mass.: Harvard University Press, 1997)
Wilde, ed. Holland	Revised version (1921) of Oscar Wilde, *The Portrait of Mr W.H.*, ed. Vyvyan Holland (London: Methuen, 1958)
Wilde, ed. Small	Original short version of Oscar Wilde, *The Portrait of Mr W.H.*, in Wilde, *Complete Short Fiction*, ed. Ian Small (Harmondsworth: Penguin Books, 1995)

A Note on Texts

Quotations and references to the Sonnets are from the Oxford edition edited by Colin Burrow or, where stated, to the 1609 Quarto. Other works by Shakespeare are quoted from the *Complete Works*, general editors Stanley Wells and Gary Taylor (Oxford, 1986). Quotations from Shakespeare's contemporaries are modernized except where there is special point in retaining the original conventions of presentation.

Fig.1. This engraving by Simon Reddick for the Folio Society edition of the Sonnets (1989) envisages a miniature portrait of a 'lovely boy' framed in a locket decorated with the intertwined initials W S and W H. The popularity during the period of the miniature as a representation of the loved one mirrors the appeal of the sonnet form; the locket, like the Sonnets, might invite exploration of its secrets.

Preface

In this book we aim to provide an introduction, overview, and guide to the reading of Shakespeare's sonnets. Underlying our objective is the belief that, individually and collectively, they are among the most accomplished and fascinating poems in the English language, that they are central to an understanding of Shakespeare's work as a poet and poetic dramatist, and that, while their autobiographical relevance is uncertain, no account of Shakespeare's outer or inner life can afford to ignore them. Expressions of variable and fluctuating friendship, love, and desire, they create the sense of an emotional reality which, while it may be illusory, unquestionably offers insight into Shakespeare's capacity to represent the imaginative states of other people, whether or not it stems directly from his personal experience.

Many myths and superstitions have accrued around these poems. The enigmatic dedication, signed with the initials of the publisher, Thomas Thorpe, not by the author, with its reference to the poems' 'onlie begetter Mr W.H.', has been the starting point for innumerable wild-goose chases. No one knows for certain when Shakespeare wrote the poems, in what order he wrote them, whether he intended them to form a single sequence, or even several different sequences, how they reached the publisher, whether Shakespeare wanted them to be published, or to whom—if indeed to any specific persons—they relate and are addressed. Though some of the first 126 poems in the collection unquestionably relate to a young man, others could relate to either a male or a female. Even the poems in the second part of the collection, known inauthentically as the 'Dark Lady' Sonnets, are not necessarily about one and the same person. The poems' relation to other verse of the time, and to Shakespeare's other writings, is uncertain because of doubts about their dates of composition.

In this book we offer no easy answers to the questions the Sonnets pose. Rather we seek to dispel the myths and to interrogate assumptions that stand in the way of an open response to the poems. With this in mind we attempt to survey critical and scholarly issues in a manner that raises, and to some extent answers, questions that may arise in the reader's mind. The prime focus of the book, however, is the poems themselves. In what ways can they be read, and what have the different possible ways of reading them—as a sequence, as groups, as individual poems, as autobiographical utterances or as dramatic monologues—to offer? What assumptions are commonly brought to bear upon them, and why? In Part I (Chapters 1 to 8) we consider the early history of Shakespeare's sonnets, their originality and artistry, and how they relate to Shakespeare's plays. Part II (Chapters 9 to 12) considers the afterlife of the Sonnets, how they have been published and received, their influence on the work of other creative writers, and the stimulus they offer to performance. In the course of our discussion we examine selected sonnets in depth, attempting to avoid the jargon of theoretical criticism along with over-technical discussion of rhetoric and prosody. The reputation of the Sonnets until the later part of the twentieth century is considered in Chapters 9 and 10; more recent critical and artistic attention is considered particularly in Chapters 9, 11, and 12. We hope that our enterprise will increase enjoyment of those of the sonnets that are frequently read, and that it will also encourage the reading of the sequence as a complexly interrelated series of poems that gain by being considered as units in a larger whole.

Part I

The Early Publication of the Sonnets

Shakespeare's sonnets as we know them were first printed as a collection in 1609, towards the end of his career. But some of them had already been offered to readers either publicly or privately. The first mention of Shakespeare as a writer of sonnets comes in *Palladis Tamia*, or *Wit's Treasury*, a book published in 1598 by the Cambridge-educated clergyman Francis Meres (1565–1647), who was well acquainted with the literary scene. The bulk of this volume is an anthology of supposedly wise sayings culled from classical and modern writers, but Meres adds a 'Comparative Discourse of our English Poets with the Greek, Latin, and Italian Poets' in which he writes admiringly of Shakespeare as both playwright and poet, saying that 'the sweet witty soul of Ovid lives in mellifluous and honey-tongued Shakespeare, witness his *Venus and Adonis*, his *Lucrece*, his sugared sonnets among his private friends, etc.'.[1] This shows that, as was common at the time, poems by Shakespeare circulated in manuscript. It does not tell us for certain whether the 'sugared sonnets' were among those that were to be printed in 1609, nor, sadly, does it name the friends who received them. But it is clear that Meres knew more of Shakespeare's writings than he could have learned of from printed sources. He refers to a number of unpublished plays, providing our only evidence of the date by which some of them could have been written.

In the following year, 1599, appeared a little book collecting twenty poems attributed to Shakespeare under the title of *The Passionate*

Pilgrim. This was an unauthorized volume put together by the publisher, William Jaggard. In fact the poems are by a variety of writers, not all of whom can now be identified, but they include three extracts from *Love's Labour's Lost*, which had already appeared in print, and which is one of the plays in which Shakespeare makes most use of the sonnet form, along with versions of what are now known as Sonnets 138 and 144. These differ from those printed in 1609 in a number of details. Once regarded as debased texts, they are now more commonly thought of as early versions of poems that Shakespeare later revised. A second edition of *The Passionate Pilgrim* of 1612, still with Shakespeare's name on the title-page, added nine poems by Thomas Heywood, who soon afterwards protested against the 'manifest injury' done to him by publishing his poems 'in a less volume, under the name of another, which may put the world in opinion I might steal them from him...But as I must acknowledge my lines not worthy his [Shakespeare's] patronage under whom he [Jaggard] hath published them, so the author I know much offended with Master Jaggard that, although unknown to him, presumed to make so bold with his name' (cited in Burrow, p. 790). No doubt as a result of this, the original title-page was replaced by one that did not mention Shakespeare.

Publication of the sonnets as a collection was heralded on 20 May 1609 by an entry in the Stationers' Register recording that the publisher Thomas Thorpe had produced his 'copy'—that is, the manuscript—for 'a book called Shakespeare's Sonnets', and had paid the company the standard fee of sixpence for authority to publish it. The book duly appeared later that year. One of its earliest purchasers was the great actor Edward Alleyn who recorded paying fivepence for a copy in June. (The authenticity of the entry has been questioned—e.g. by Duncan-Jones, p. 7—unnecessarily, in our view.) The Quarto's title-page proclaims that the volume contains 'Shakespeare's Sonnets. Never before Imprinted.' The wording is unusual; a more common formula would have been for the volume to bear a title naming an addressee, followed perhaps by the author's name. 'Shakespeare's Sonnets' is, as it were, in the third person; this is not an author offering his poems to the public but a publisher boasting that he is at last able to offer to the public poems long known to exist but 'never before imprinted'. Shakespeare was well known; by this date he had written about thirty plays, some of which had appeared in print in one or more

Fig. 2. In June 1609, only weeks after the Sonnets first appeared in print, the great actor Edward Alleyn recorded buying a copy in a list of accounts (under the heading 'Houshowld stuff'): 'a book Shaksper sonetts 5d'. Some Shakespeare scholars dispute the authenticity of the entry, attributing it to the nineteenth-century forger John Payne Collier; but Collier scholars deny that it is an authentic forgery.

editions with his name on the title-page. Even more relevantly to readers of poetry, he was renowned as the writer of the immensely popular comic and erotic narrative poem *Venus and Adonis* and its tragic counterpart *The Rape of Lucrece*. New work by a popular poet and dramatist who had published almost no verses (the exception is 'The Phoenix and Turtle', or 'Let the Bird of Loudest Lay', which appeared in 1601) for fifteen years might well have attracted attention.

Turning over the title-page, an early reader would have found a dedication which is also unusual in coming from the publisher, not the author. Whereas *Venus and Adonis* and *The Rape of Lucrece*, first published in 1593 and 1594, both carried dedications to the Earl of Southampton printed over the author's name, the Sonnets has only a

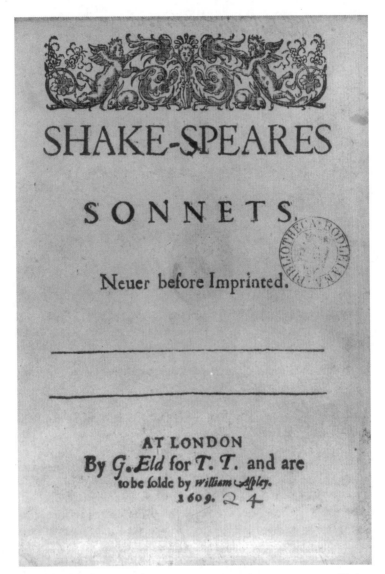

Fig. 3. The title-page of the 1609 Quarto gives high prominence to Shakespeare's name and to the fact that the sonnets had not previously been printed.

brief inscription printed over the initials of the publisher. The curious layout is that of a Roman inscription, perhaps intended to dignify the book with the appearance of learning. Again the volume is being presented in the third person. The phrasing seems designed to conceal more than it reveals. And indeed few if any sentences ever written have given rise to more speculation. The author is alive, so why did he not write his own dedication? Who is Mr W.H.? Why is his name not given in full? In what sense did he 'beget' the poems?—does it mean that he wrote them, or inspired them, or commissioned them, or procured the manuscript for the publisher? The wish that the dedicatee may enjoy 'that eternity promised by our ever-living poet' reflects the content of those sonnets in which the poet declares that he is conferring immortality upon his beloved, but like the poems themselves, the dedication confers only a nameless immortality. There is a touch of wit in the words 'setting forth', which pun on the senses 'going to sea', meaning that the publisher's enterprise resembles the start of a merchant adventurer's journey, and on 'setting' the poems 'forth' in print.

The third-person aspects of the publication raise the question of whether the volume appeared by Shakespeare's desire or whether Thorpe got hold of a manuscript without authority. As we have seen, Shakespeare had suffered from piracy in *The Passionate Pilgrim*, whose publisher, William Jaggard, must directly or indirectly have acquired manuscripts of two sonnets from one of the 'private friends' to whom they had been entrusted. Thorpe was a reputable publisher, and we have no record that Shakespeare objected to his publishing the Sonnets. But the fact that they had not appeared before 1609, long after the vogue for sonnet sequences was over, along with the evidence that at least some of them were over ten years old, suggests that Shakespeare had not primarily intended them for publication, and the absence of evidence that he was associated with their appearance in 1609 leaves open the possibility that it was not by his desire. It seems strange that he did not write the dedication himself unless, as Katherine Duncan-Jones (pp. 11–12) has conjectured, he was simply out of London at the time, perhaps evading the plague. Even if this is true he might have been expected to supply preliminary matter along with the copy; or indeed publication might have been delayed till his return.

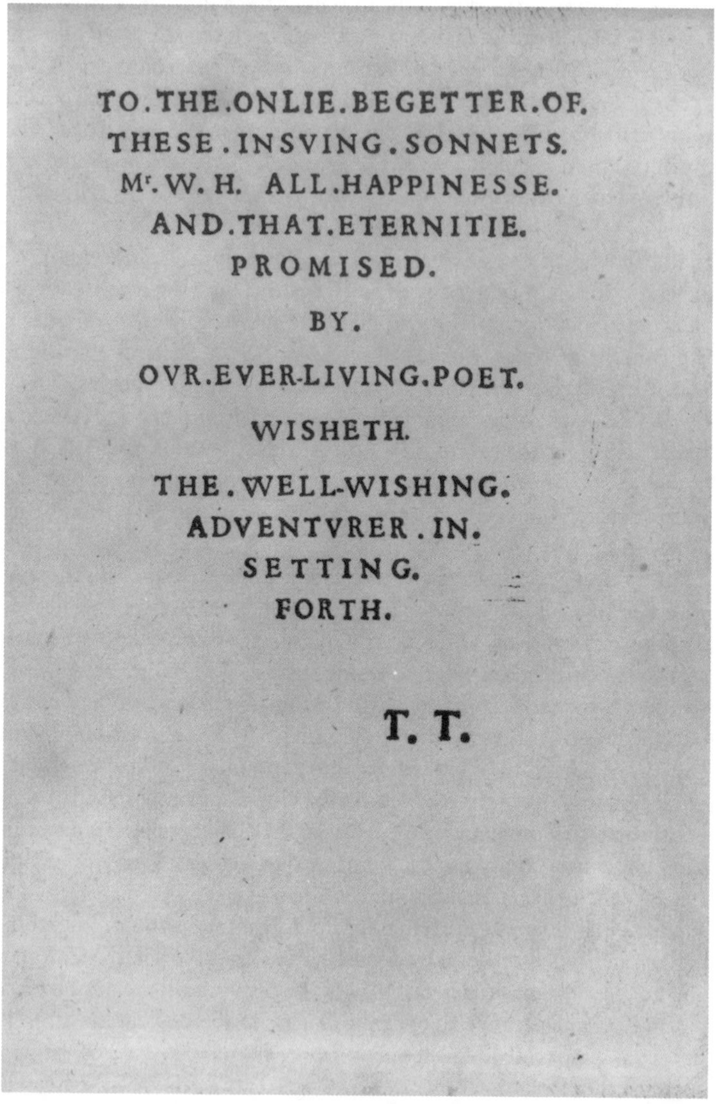

TO.THE.ONLIE.BEGETTER.OF.
THESE.INSVING.SONNETS.
M^r.W.H. ALL.HAPPINESSE.
AND.THAT.ETERNITIE.
PROMISED.

BY.

OVR.EVER-LIVING.POET.

WISHETH.

THE.WELL-WISHING.
ADVENTVRER.IN.
SETTING.
FORTH.

T. T.

Fig. 4. This dedication page of the 1609 Quarto, signed with the initials of
the publisher, Thomas Thorpe, has provoked discussion of its layout, its
phrasing, and above all the identity of 'M^r. W. H.'

The volume that Thorpe set forth is made up first of 154 numbered poems. Normally each page has thirty-six lines of type. The poems run over the page breaks with more concern for economy than for aesthetics or sense, to such an extent that even the first line of two of the sonnets (Nos. 101 and 137) is followed by a page break. All but three are in what had come to be regarded as the standard sonnet form: fourteen-line poems in iambic pentameters with a clearly defined rhyme scheme, most usually abab cdcd efef gg. This is the form of most of the sonnets published during the great vogue for the form, in the 1590s, but in them as in the Shakespeare collection it is not invariable. Many of the sequences include non-standard poems, and John Donne's *Songs and Sonnets*, written and circulated in the early seventeenth century but not published until 1633, contains not a single fourteen-line poem. There are three structural anomalies in Shakespeare's collection. Sonnet 99 has fifteen lines to convey its conceit that the 'forward violet' and other flowers have stolen their 'sweet or colour' from the lover—hence the extra, introductory line (made possible by an 'ababa' rhyme scheme at the beginning). Sonnet 126 (discussed on pp. 29–31, below) is made up entirely of rhyming couplets. Sonnet 145 is formally different because it is composed in iambic tetrameter. This, coupled with the possible pun on 'hate away' and 'Hathaway' (Shakespeare's wife's maiden name) in the couplet, might make it a much earlier work than the rest of the collection. It might even be the first mature poem Shakespeare composed.

The 154 sonnets are followed by the poem 'A Lover's Complaint' which has a separate attribution to 'William Shakespeare'. This narrative poem, written in the seven-line stanza form known as rhyme royal, which Shakespeare also uses in *The Rape of Lucrece*, is discussed in Chapter 8, below.

Careful analysis of the text printed by Thorpe has made it possible for scholars to make educated guesses about the nature of the manuscript that Thorpe showed to the wardens of the Stationers' Company and that his workmen used in the printing house. If this manuscript was in Shakespeare's hand the printed version would lie at only one remove from the author, and so would have a better chance of representing him accurately than if it had passed through additional stages. It was common in this period for compositors to repunctuate

129

TH'expence of Spirit in a wafte of fhame
Is luft in action, and till action, luft
Is periurd, murdrous, blouddy full of blame,
Sauage, extreame, rude, cruell, not to truft,
Inioyd no fooner but difpifed ftraight,
Paft reafon hunted, and no fooner had
Paft reafon hated as a fwollowed bayt,
On purpofe layd to make the taker mad.
Made In purfut and in poffeffion fo,
Had, hauing, and in queft, to haue extreame,
A bliffe in proofe and proud and very wo,
Before a ioy propofd behind a dreame,
     All this the world well knowes yet none knowes well,
     To fhun the heauen that leads men to this hell.

Fig. 5. The original printing of Sonnet 129 illustrates some of the problems that face an editor in modernizing incidentals of presentation such as spelling, punctuation, and capitalization.

what they set up in print, and to diverge from their manuscript in other ways that should not, but sometimes did, affect meaning. The Sonnets were set into type by two different workmen, each of whom uses an individual style of punctuation, so clearly the punctuation of the poems cannot be relied on to reflect Shakespeare's own. MacDonald P. Jackson has shown that twenty of the sixty-five Quarto pages can be attributed to one compositor, and forty-five to another. Variables include whether or not the third quatrain ends with a colon or a full stop and the frequency with which each compositor uses a question mark.[2] And it is revealing that the word 'thy' is misprinted some fourteen times as 'their' (e.g. Sonnet 46, l. 8, 'And says in him their fair appearance lyes', and twice in ll. 13–14, 'As thus, mine eyes due is their outward part, | And my hearts right, their inward loue of heart'), and that this error occurs in the work of both men. This suggests that whoever wrote the underlying manuscript formed his letters in a way that encouraged this misreading. The fact that it has not been found anywhere else in Shakespeare's work makes it reasonable to suppose that Thorpe's manuscript was a transcript made by someone other than the author. Perhaps Shakespeare had commissioned a scribe to prepare a copy for presentation to a patron or friend. Or perhaps some third person had transcribed such a copy.

A shred of evidence supporting this theory is the presence of Shakespeare's name beneath the title of 'A Lover's Complaint', another third-person identification that would have been unnecessary in the author's own copy. It is likely then that the Sonnets were printed from a manuscript that was not penned by Shakespeare himself.

For all this, the book includes relatively few apparent mistakes. The most conspicuous is at the start of Sonnet 146, where the original has

> Poore soule the center of my sinfull earth,
> My sinfull earth these rebell powres that thee array...

The unmetrical repetition is generally considered to be an error (though it has been, rather tortuously, defended). Most editors replace the repeated words with empty space, but well over eighty different attempts to supply the supposedly missing words are recorded; among the more plausible are 'Rebuke', 'Fooled by [those]', 'Feeding these', and 'Sieged by these'.[3]

Although then the Quarto text as a whole is fairly reliable, its original presentation poses many problems for the modern reader. Spelling, punctuation, capitalization, and use of italics frequently differ from modern usage. In modern editions it is customary to regularize the texts, attempting to interpret the poems through a modern orthographical and typographical lens. This requires many delicate decisions, and may at times result in the ironing out of potentially fruitful ambiguities. Take for example Sonnet 129, as printed in the Quarto (see fig. 5).

Some words here—such as 'murdrous', 'extreame', 'dispised', 'swollowed', 'pursut'—are easily enough rendered into their modern form. Others are more disputable. In the first line, 'waste' may be regarded as a variant spelling of 'waist', may have conveyed that meaning to an early reader, and could convey both senses to a modern hearer. In the phrase 'blouddy full of blame' a modern editor is likely to place a comma between 'bloody' and 'full'. At the beginning of line 9 'Made' is most naturally understood as a spelling of 'mad', but has (improbably, in our view) been defended. The most difficult phrase is 'and proud and very wo'. As we see in other words here—'Sauage', 'hauing'—the letter u was often used within a word where we would use v. In conjunction with the word 'proofe' the most likely meaning for 'proud' here is 'proved'; this has led most editors to take the second 'and' to be a misprint for 'a': 'and proved a very woe', that is, 'having been experienced, a source of real misery'.

Even after decisions about presentation have been made, many ambiguities and meanings unavailable to the untutored modern reader may remain. Meanings of words have shifted, contracted, or expanded, some more conspicuously than others. In the first line, for instance, the word 'Spirit' could mean 'semen'. 'Rude' (l. 4) has reduced in strength. In the same line, 'to trust' means 'to be trusted'. In line 10, the phrase 'in quest, to haue extreme' may be understood as 'in quest to have, extreme'.

Clearly, then, a modern reader cannot expect to understand the original text without help, but re-presentation will inevitably result in a degree of simplification which may even extend so far as misrepresentation. There is no avoiding this, and whilst the use of a responsibly modernized edition may alert the reader to alternative significances, it is crucial that we as readers remain alert to the nature of the edition we are using. Modern editions are discussed in some detail in Chapter 9.

The History and Emergence of the Sonnet as a Literary Form

In Shakespeare's comedy *The Merry Wives of Windsor*, written probably around 1597, at the height of popularity of the English sonnet sequence, young Abraham Slender, seeking inspiration in his wooing of Anne Page, declares 'I had rather than forty shillings I had my book of songs and sonnets here' (1.1.181–2). He is speaking of the first English poetry anthology, the *Songs and Sonnets* published in 1557 by Richard Tottel, and now generally known as *Tottel's Miscellany*. This is a substantial collection of sonnets and other lyrical poems, many of them written by Sir Thomas Wyatt (1503–42) and Henry Howard, Earl of Surrey (?1517–47), which had previously circulated only in manuscript. It was reprinted within a couple of months of its first appearance, and successive revisions had continued to give solace and encouragement to wooers, probably including Shakespeare, in at least eight more editions by 1587.

The popularity of this volume is largely responsible for bringing into the mainstream of English verse a poetic form that had come into prominence during the fourteenth century in Italy in the work of Dante Alighieri (1265–1321) and, especially, Francesco Petrarch (1304–74). Their sequences, like those of many of their successors, were interspersed with poems in other metrical and stanzaic forms. Petrarch was known in England during his lifetime—his younger contemporary Geoffrey Chaucer (*c*.1343–1400) translates one of his sonnets (though not in sonnet form) in his long narrative poem *Troilus and Criseyde* and refers to him admiringly in *The Clerk's Tale*.

Still, the vogue that Dante and Petrarch had initiated did not take on international dimensions until the sixteenth century, when sonnet sequences became immensely popular in, especially, Spain, France, and, finally, England. In mid-century France the sonnet, often in translation and adaptation from both Italian and classical models, was the favoured form of Pierre Ronsard (1524–85), Joachim du Bellay (1522–60), and other members of the group of poets known as the Pléiade. Wyatt and Surrey, too, drew heavily on Italian models, especially Petrarch; the English poets' sonnets are only loosely interrelated.

It was not, however, until 1591, with the posthumous publication of Sir Philip Sidney's *Astrophil and Stella*, that the English vogue for collections and sequences of sonnets, often interspersed with poems in other lyric forms, and sometimes followed, like Shakespeare's, by a verse complaint, really took off. During the next seven years at least nineteen such collections, mostly amorous in subject matter and of very varying quality, appeared in print, and several others were written but not published. Among their authors are Sir Philip Sidney (*Astrophil and Stella*, written by 1586, posthumously published in 1591), Samuel Daniel (*Delia*, 1592), Barnabe Barnes (*Parthenophil and Parthenophe*, 1593; *A Divine Century of Spiritual Sonnets*, 1595), Thomas Lodge (*Phillis*, 1593), Giles Fletcher (*Licia*, 1593), Thomas Watson (*The Tears of Fancy, or Love Disdained*, 1593), Henry Constable (*Diana*, 1594), Michael Drayton (*Idea's Mirror*, 1594), William Percy (*Sonnets to . . . Celia*, 1594), Edmund Spenser, *Amoretti* (1595), Bartholomew Griffin (*Fidessa*, 1596), Richard Linche, *Diella* (1596), William Smith (*Chloris*, 1596), Richard Barnfield, *Cynthia* (1597), and Robert Tofte, *Laura* (1597). One conspicuous difference from Shakespeare's poems is that almost all these collections have titles, and that almost all the titles include the name or pseudonym of a woman. Shakespeare's collection is the longest by almost 50 per cent (Sidney's comes second, with 108 sonnets). Early in the seventeenth century the emphasis shifted to religious sonnets, and by the time Shakespeare's sonnets were printed, in 1609, the vogue for love sonnets was already out of fashion. This may help to explain why Shakespeare's collection was not reprinted until 1640, and then in garbled form, as we shall see in Chapter 9.

There is no question that Petrarch exerted a colossal influence on the English sonnet in general, and on Shakespeare in particular, if indirectly and, at times, obliquely. The influence on Shakespeare extends beyond his own poems in sonnet form to other poems and plays. He refers directly to the Italian poet in *Romeo and Juliet* when Mercutio, mocking the lovesick Romeo, says 'Now is he for the numbers that Petrarch flowed in. Laura'—Petrarch's idealized addressee—compared 'to his lady was a kitchen wench—marry she had a better love to berhyme her...' (2.3.36–8); and the whole portrayal of Romeo's relationship to the unseen Rosaline mirrors Petrarch's relationship with Laura. Shakespeare proclaims his independence from convention in Sonnet 130 in which, while declaring love for his mistress, he mocks the standard vocabulary of praise:

> My mistress' eyes are nothing like the sun,
> Coral is far more red than her lips' red.
> If snow be white, why then her breasts are dun,
> If hairs be wires, black wires grow on her head....
>
> (ll. 1–4)

Dissociating himself from convention here, Shakespeare nevertheless is indebted to previous practitioners; in writing these lines he may have had in mind as objects of parody specific poems by writers including Richard Barnfield, Bartholomew Griffin, Henry Constable, Richard Linche, and especially Thomas Watson in the following poem from his *Hekatompathia* of 1582:

> Hark you that list to hear what saint I serve:
> Her yellow locks exceed the beaten gold;
> Her sparkling eyes in heaven a place deserve;
> Her forehead high and fair of comely mould;
> Her words are music all of silver sound;
> Her wit so sharp as like can scarce be found:
> Each eyebrow hangs like Iris in the skies;
> Her eagle's nose is straight of stately flame;
> Her lips more red than any coral stone;
> Her neck more white, than aged swans that moan;
> Her breast transparent is, like crystal rock;
> Her fingers long, fit for Apollo's lute;
> Her slipper such as Momus dare not mock;

> Her virtues all so great as make me mute:
> What other parts she hath I need not say,
> Whose face alone is cause of my decay.
>
> (Sonnet 7)

The fundamental premiss of the Petrarchan sonnet is simple: a man loves and desires a beautiful woman who is dedicated to chastity, which may be either virginity or the 'married chastity' that Shakespeare celebrates in his poem beginning 'Let the Bird of Loudest Lay' (usually known as 'The Phoenix and Turtle'). Romeo expresses the idea to Benvolio:

> She'll not be hit
> With Cupid's arrow; she hath Dian's wit,
> And, in strong proof of chastity well armed,
> From love's weak childish bow she lives unharmed.
> She will not stay the siege of loving terms,
> Or bide th'encounter of assailing eyes,
> Nor ope her lap to saint-seducing gold.
> O, she is rich in beauty, only poor
> That when she dies, with beauty dies her store.
>
> (*Romeo and Juliet*, 1.1.205–13)

It is only a short step from that to the encouragements to breed in the opening sonnets of Shakespeare's volume. But they are addressed by a man to a man.

By contrast, almost all the English sonnets of Shakespeare's time are addressed by a man to a woman whom the man idealizes as Romeo idealizes Rosaline. But as, among the Italian poets, Michelangelo addressed love poems to men, so in England too there are just a few exceptions to the general rule, in the work of Richard Barnfield (1574–1620), who is one of the first writers to mention Shakespeare in print. This is in a poem headed 'A Remembrance of Some English Poets', published in 1598, where he writes:

> And Shakespeare thou, whose honey-flowing vein,
> Pleasing the world, thy praises doth obtain;
> Whose *Venus* and whose *Lucrece*—sweet and chaste—
> Thy name in fame's immortal book have placed;

> Live ever you, at least in fame live ever.
> Well may the body die, but fame dies never.
>
> > (Barnfield, p. 182)

One of Barnfield's longer poems, published in 1594 when he was around 20 years old and written in the same stanza form as *Venus and Adonis*, is 'The Tears of an Affectionate Shepherd Sick for Love; or The Complaint of Daphnis for the Love of Ganymede'. This is sensuously erotic in a manner that far exceeds any of the sonnet sequences addressed to women, more conspicuously resembling Marlowe's homoeroticism in *Hero and Leander* (written by 1593 and circulated in manuscript, but not published until 1598) and *Edward II*, which had just been printed. Barnfield, whose poems are variously indebted to Marlowe, quotes an entire line from the play: 'Crownets of pearl about [thy *for* his] naked arms' (1.1.63): probably he had been keen to buy a copy hot from the press. Daphnis addresses Ganymede in lines wide open to homoerotic interpretation:

> O would to God, so I could have my fee,
> My lips were honey, and thy mouth a bee.
> Then shouldst thou suck my sweet and my fair flower
>
> That now is ripe and full of honey berries;
> Then would I lead thee to my pleasant bower
> Filled full of grapes, of mulberries and cherries.
>
> > (Barnfield, p. 82)

And later:

> And every morn by dawning of the day
> > When Phoebus riseth with a blushing face
> Silvanus' chapel clerks shall chant a lay,
> > And play thee hunt's up in thy resting place.
> My cot thy chamber, my bosom thy bed,
> Shall be appointed for thy sleepy head.
>
> > (Barnfield, p. 82)

This is pretty explicit, and it seems to have got Barnfield into trouble, because in the dedication to his next book, *Cynthia, with Certain Sonnets and the Legend of Cassandra* (1595), he defends himself against the accusation that some 'did interpret *The Affectionate Shepherd* otherwise than in truth I meant, touching the subject thereof, to wit, the love of a shepherd to a boy', on the grounds that his poem was 'nothing else but an imitation of Virgil, in the second Eclogue of Alexis' (Barnfield, pp. 115–16). But in fact the resemblance to Virgil is slight; and the new volume includes a sequence of, this time, sonnets also concerned with Ganymede which are explicitly and unashamedly homoerotic, full of physical desire:

> Sometimes I wish that I his pillow were,
>   So might I steal a kiss, and yet not seen.
>   So might I gaze upon his sleeping eyne,
> Although I did it with a panting fear.
> But when I well consider how vain my wish is,
>   'Ah, foolish bees', think I, 'that do not suck
>   His lips for honey, but poor flowers do pluck
> Which have no sweet in them, when his sole kisses
> Are able to revive a dying soul.
>   Kiss him, but sting him not, for if you do
>   His angry voice your flying will pursue.'
> But when they hear his tongue, what can control
>   Their back return? For then they plain may see
>   How honeycombs from his lips dropping be.
>
> (Barnfield, p. 126)

The poet's love, we learn, is unrequited; when he confesses that he is in love, his friend assumes that he loves a woman:

> . . . what is she . . . whom thou dost love?

To which the poet, taking up a covered mirror, responds:

> 'Look in this glass', quoth I, 'there shalt thou see
>   The perfect form of my felicity.'
> When, thinking that it would strange magic prove,
>   He opened it, and taking off the cover
> He straight perceived himself to be my lover.
>
> (Barnfield, p. 127)

Barnfield is likely to have known Shakespeare personally, and was influenced in his poetry by Shakespeare's *Venus and Adonis*. The tone of the two poets' poems is very different, but Paul Hammond (*Figuring Sex*, pp. 72–84) has convincingly demonstrated that Shakespeare engaged with poems by Barnfield in his sonnets. And it is interesting that one other love poet of the period, whether before, after, or along with Shakespeare, wrote poems to a male. Barnfield's action in doing so, or the attitude of mind that lay behind it, may have been responsible for his being regarded as the black sheep of his family; it was discovered in 1991 that he was disinherited in favour of his younger brother.[1]

While it is relatively easy to place Shakespeare's sonnets in relation to the sonnet tradition before Sir Philip Sidney, his relationship with the great period of English sonnet sequences is more problematical. This is partly because, though we can hazard a guess about the date of a few of Shakespeare's individual sonnets, it is far from easy to determine when the bulk of them were written, and when he—if he it was—assembled them as what is better thought of as a collection than a sequence, since, as we discuss in Chapter 4, the individual poems do not hang together from beginning to end as a single unity. So, though there are resemblances between Shakespeare's collection and others by poets including Samuel Daniel, in his sequence *Delia*, we cannot be sure which way the influence operated. What we can say for certain is that Shakespeare is far less dependent on Continental models than, for instance, Michael Drayton or most other sonneteers of the period. The idea that the average sonneteer looked in his heart and wrote, as Philip Sidney declares, in the first poem of *Astrophil and Stella*, that his Muse bade him do, could not be further from the truth. Sidney Lee, writing of the 'wholesale loans which the Elizabethan sonneteers invariably levied on foreign literature', remarks that 'genuine originality of thought and expression was rare' (Lee, p. xxxiv). Some of them, he continues, 'prove, when their work is compared with that of foreign writers, to have been verbatim translators, and almost sink to the level of literary pirates'. Giles Fletcher's *Licia*, published in 1593, at least has the honesty to announce on its title-page that these 'poems of love in honour of the admirable and singular virtues of his lady', as he calls them, so far from being personal outpourings, are written in 'imitation of the best Latin poets and others' (cited in Lee, p. 23). Licia, Fletcher teasingly writes, may be a mere abstraction, perhaps 'learning's image, or some heavenly wonder…perhaps under that name I have shadowed "[the holy] discipline"', or perhaps 'that kind courtesy which I found at the patroness of these poems', or 'some college' (he had been a Fellow of King's College Cambridge), or 'it may be my conceit and pretend nothing' (cited in Lee, p. 32). 'A man may write of love and not be in love, as well as of husbandry and not go to the plough, or of witches and be none, or of holiness and be flat profane' (cited in Lee, p. 28). Is this deliberate obfuscation, we may ask, a playful attempt to deflect enquiry into a living object of love? The depth of Giles Fletcher's indebtedness to Continental and other models suggests not: suggests in fact that his sonnets are, as Shakespeare's have often been described, literary exercises largely divorced from personal experience.

In the meantime we can say with certainty that Shakespeare's sonnets are quite exceptional in their relationship to other sequences, in their overall lack of indebtedness to direct models, as well as in their frequent defiance of conventions of the genre. Like all his work, they reflect his reading. Erasmus's 'Epistle to persuade a young man to marriage' appears, directly or indirectly, to have influenced the arguments in favour of procreation in the first group of sonnets (Burrow, note to Sonnet 1)—in any case this was a commonplace literary theme, evident for example in Marlowe's *Hero and Leander* and used by Shakespeare in a ribald passage of dialogue on virginity in *All's Well that Ends Well* (1.1.105–61). Sonnet 60 is clearly related to lines in Ovid's *Metamorphoses*, in which the philosopher Pythagoras, meditating on change, says, in the Elizabethan translation by Arthur Golding:

> look
> As every wave drives other forth, and that that comes behind
> Both thrusteth and is thrust itself: even so the times by kind
> Do fly and follow both at once, and evermore renew.
> For that that was before is left, and straight there doth ensue
> Another that was never erst. Each twinkling of an eye
> Doth change.
>
> (bk. 15, ll. 200–6)

So in Sonnet 60 Shakespeare writes:

> Like as the waves make towards the pebbled shore,
> So do our minutes hasten to their end,

> Each changing place with that which goes before,
> In sequent toil all forwards do contend.

(ll. 1–4)

Sonnet 114, in the phrase 'things indigest' (l. 5), recalls the opening of the *Metamorphoses*: 'chaos: rudis indigesta moles' (1. 7): 'chaos, a rude and shapeless mass', and Sonnet 63 has links with another passage from the *Metamorphoses* in its meditation on the likely effects of 'time's injurious hand' (l. 2) on the beloved's beauty.

It seems significant that Shakespeare's clearest borrowing comes in two of the least typical, and least admired, of his sonnets, those placed last, Nos. 153 and 154, which play variations on a single passage, deriving ultimately but by some unknown route from the following ancient Greek epigram by Marianus Scholasticus, a poet of the fifth and sixth centuries AD:

Beneath these plane trees, detained by gentle slumber, Love slept, having put his torch in the care of the Nymphs; but the Nymphs said to one another 'Why wait? Would that together with this we could quench the fire in the hearts of men.' But the torch set fire even to the water, and with hot water thenceforth the Love-Nymphs fill the bath. (Burrow, note to Sonnet 153)

This source seems to dispose effectively of the common notion that Shakespeare's sonnets refer to the town of Bath, and (unless Shakespeare is finding the possibilities for puns that go beyond his source) makes it less likely that they refer to treatments for venereal disease.

So, though Shakespeare's sonnets, like all his work, unquestionably reflect his reading, and though not all of them are intimate in tone, it is not unreasonable to look in them for reflections of his personal experience.

The Sonnets in Relation to
Shakespeare's Life

Perhaps more than any other text in Western literature, Shakespeare's sonnets have inspired a multiplicity of controversially biographical readings. All of these take as their central assumption the hypothesis that the 'I' of the Sonnets ineluctably represents Shakespeare's point of view and so gives direct access to scenes and events of his life. Any attempt to relate a work of art directly to the intimate, personal life of the artist needs to be treated with caution, even suspicion. This said, it is natural that those who believe that a real-life story lies behind Shakespeare's sonnets should seek to identify the participants. Success in doing so might illuminate details of their phrasing and add to knowledge of Shakespeare's biography. On the other hand attempts at identification have been so inconclusive, and often fantastic, that here we shall do no more than outline some of the more prominent theories.

The usual assumption has been that there were only four participants: the poet himself; a young man featured in the first 126 poems; a 'black', or dark, woman with whom many of the remainder are concerned; and a poet alluded to with various degrees of clarity in Sonnets 78–80 and 82–6 who was a rival with the poet for the young man's love. But in 1971, in an article in *Essays in Criticism*, A. J. Gurr plausibly suggested that Sonnet 145, with its puns on 'hate' and 'away', is a love lyric addressed to Anne Hathaway, whom Shakespeare had wooed, impregnated, and wed by 1581. It is set off from the rest of the collection by its irregular form: though it has fourteen lines and uses the standard rhyme scheme, it is composed in octosyllabics, not iambic pentameters. If the collection could include one poem written early in Shakespeare's career, it could include others written at any point until the volume went to press. In theory, at least, this means that sonnets may have been addressed to more than one young man, and even to more than one 'dark lady'. (Whether Anne was dark we don't know.) Thorpe's dedication to the 'only begetter of these ensuing sonnets' suggests a single addressee and that he is thinking of a man; on the other hand if we take 'begetter' to mean 'inspirer' there were clearly at least two of them, a man and a woman; and the possibility that the Sonnets had a number of addressees is implicit in the statement in Sonnet 31 that the 'I' of the poem had had a sequence of lovers: 'Thou art the grave where buried love doth live, | Hung with the trophies of my lovers gone, | Who all their parts of me to thee did give; | That due of many, | Now is thine alone' (ll. 9–12).

The idea even that the poet is Shakespeare writing in his own person has often been resisted. In part this denial derives from bardolatrous resistance to the thought that Shakespeare could have been the kind of man—adulterously involved with a promiscuous woman, and possibly a lover of men as well as of women—that the Sonnets seem to imply. At the very least we can say that, as Paul Hammond puts it, 'Shakespeare, obviously deeply committed emotionally and imaginatively to the subject, though for reasons which we can no longer trace, created a sequence of poems which explore the delight and despair which may attend one man's love for another' (*Love between Men*, p. 77).

The case that Shakespeare does not personally mean what his poetic persona says has been supported by allusions that may seem to point away from him, such as references to himself as an old man— 'That time of year thou mayst in me behold | When yellow leaves, or none, or few do hang | Upon those boughs which shake against the cold' (Sonnet 73, ll. 1–3)—though Shakespeare was only 45 years old when the poems appeared, and younger when most of them were written. This may be mere self-dramatization. And the wordplay on Shakespeare's first name, Will[iam], in, especially, Sonnets 135 and 136, along with the explicit statement 'my name is Will' (No. 136), seems like clear self-identification. It has been proposed that in the first seventeen sonnets he was writing not on personal impulse but to commission on behalf of a patron who sought to persuade a young man, probably his or her son, to marry; in other sonnets he may have been writing love poems on someone else's behalf. Such a patron or sponsor is unlikely to have thanked him, let alone paid him, for some of the 'Dark Lady' sonnets. But there is a sense in which any poet is adopting a persona—even poets do not normally express their everyday thoughts in rhymed and structured verse. As John Kerrigan writes in the fine introduction to his edition, 'Shakespeare stands behind the first person of his sequence as Sidney had stood behind Astrophil—sometimes near the poetic "I", sometimes farther off, but never without some degree of rhetorical projection' (Kerrigan, p. 11). Oscar Wilde expressed a similar sentiment when he wrote, in *The Portrait of Mr W.H.* (see p. 140, below), of all art as 'an attempt to realise one's own personality on some imaginative plane out of reach of the trammelling accidents and limitations of real life' (Wilde, ed. Holland, p. 3). To write a poem, however heartfelt it may be, is to adopt a stance which distances the writer from spontaneity of utterance, even while trying to express deeper truths than can be conveyed in the language of ordinary speech. We can never know how much of Shakespeare's collection reflects his personal point of view, and if he were here to discuss the poems with modern readers, he would probably discover meanings that he had not been aware of. Even explicitly dramatic soliloquies such as those written by Robert Browning convey, however obliquely, something of the poet's own point of view.

　　Attempts to identify the young man have centred on the assumption that he is the 'Mr'—i.e. Master—'W. H.' of Thorpe's dedication, and that Thorpe's 'only begetter' means 'sole inspirer'. (A less likely possibility is 'only procurer of the manuscript'.) The established fact that Shakespeare dedicated his narrative poems to Henry Wriothesley has encouraged speculation that 'W.H.' is a deliberately cryptic inversion of the Earl's initials, with the added smokescreen of referring to him as a commoner. This would mean that the dedication was comprehensible only to the selected few. But W.H., uninverted, are the initials of William Herbert, Earl of Pembroke (1580–1630), dedicatee along with his brother Philip of the First Folio. Certainly, on the evidence of the sonnets that pun on the name Will (Nos. 135–6 and, less certainly, 143), a William seems more likely than a Henry. But

Herbert, too, was not properly addressed as M[aste]r, and he was embarrassingly young at the time that the earliest sonnets may have been written. Another candidate is Sir William Harvey, Southampton's stepfather, on the grounds that he might have been able to get hold of the manuscript and to pass it on to Thorpe. Some critics suppose that W.H. stands for William Himself, or is a misprint for W.S., and that Thorpe is dedicating his poems to their author. There is no way of either proving or disproving these convenient hypotheses, any more than the suggestion that W.H. means Who He?, awkwardly modern though this locution might appear to be.

Looking for internal evidence, the eighteenth-century scholar Edmond Malone took his cue from Sonnet 20: 'a man in hue all hues in his controlling', which he supposed to be a pun on the name Hughes. This idea was most famously, if not entirely seriously, espoused by Oscar Wilde in his short story *The Portrait of Mr W.H.* (1889, later revised), where he fantasized that Hughes was 'a wonderful boy-actor of great beauty' (Wilde, ed. Small, p. 57). And the novelist Samuel Butler succeeded in finding a real-life William Hughes who was appointed cook on a ship called *The Vanguard* in 1634 and who was dead two years later. The plethora of candidates—many more could be named—suggests that if Thorpe's use of initials was intended to conceal the truth from all but a selected band of readers in his own time he must be congratulated on his success.

What of the woman—or women—in the case? A few clues appear in the poems—she (if there was only one) was both literally and metaphorically 'dark', in whatever sense of the word, was married but promiscuous, and could play a keyboard instrument (Sonnet 131). Hundreds, if not thousands, of Elizabethan women could have fitted this bill. George Chalmers, reacting to his literary enemy Edmond Malone, proposed in 1797 that not only the last group, but all the sonnets were addressed to Queen Elizabeth (who could play the virginals but was neither dark nor married), explaining that she was often thought of as a man. He expressed astonishment at the very notion that 'Shakespeare, a husband, a father, a moral man, addressed a hundred and twenty, nay, a hundred and twenty-six *Amourous* Sonnets to a *male* object'.[1] Chalmers got into a terrible tangle trying to explain how Sonnet 20, with its puns on 'prick', might have been addressed to the Queen. A popular candidate during the late

nineteenth century was Mary Fitton, one of Elizabeth's maids of honour (see pp. 141–2, below), but her star waned when she was discovered to have been fair. Jane (or Jennet) Davenant has been a natural suspect in view of hints by her son William, the dramatist (1606–8) who adapted several of Shakespeare's plays for the Restoration stage, that Shakespeare was his father. The twentieth-century scholar G. B. Harrison, believing the woman to have been black-skinned, proposed a prostitute named Lucy Morgan; in 1973 A. L. Rowse trumpeted his belief that she was Emilia Lanier, who was certainly the mistress of the Lord Chamberlain, Lord Hunsdon, and came of a musical family, but her darkness fell from the air when it was shown that she was not, as Rowse, misreading his manuscript sources, claimed in *Shakespeare the Man* (1973), 'brown' but 'brave in youth'. In spite of this Michael Wood (who also implausibly finds signs of Shakespeare's son Hamnet, who died at the age of 11, in Sonnet 33) espouses her cause in his *Shakespeare: His Life and Times* (2003). All these theories assume that any such 'dark lady' has naturally left good documentary evidence as to her existence and identity; Shakespeare's lovers have probably left not a wrack behind them, apart from the Sonnets, and then only if the poems represent some kind of autobiography. The case will always remain open.

Even more tenuous are claims to identify the poet (or poets) who, according to Sonnets 78–80 and 81–6, was a rival in the sonneteer's love. He wielded a 'worthier pen' (Sonnet 79, l. 6) than the author, and is 'a better spirit' to whom the poet is 'inferior far'. Sonnet 86 speaks of 'the proud full sail' of his 'great verse', and conjectures that 'his spirit' was 'by spirits taught to write | Above a mortal pitch' (ll. 1–6). And he has a mysterious 'affable familiar ghost | Which nightly gulls him with intelligence' (ll. 9–10). Worst of all, the fair young man's 'countenance filled up' the rival's 'line', depriving the poet of 'matter' (ll. 13–14). Almost every poet of Shakespeare's time, including Spenser, Marlowe, Chapman, and Jonson, as well as some poets of other times, has been proposed by scholars with a taste for proving the unprovable.

More important than what the Sonnets tell us about Shakespeare's contemporaries is the evidence they may provide about his personality. Other chapters of this book touch on some aspects of this subject. It goes without saying that the Sonnets are the work of a master craftsman who had thought long and deeply about his art. Study of his

artistry (Chapter 5) may provide insights into his creative processes. Analysis of the Sonnets' subject matter (Chapter 6) tells us about his preoccupations within these poems, though our views may fluctuate according to whether we consider them to spring directly from his own experience or to have been shaped in part or in whole by other factors such as the desire to project imaginary situations, possibly at the behest of patrons. And study of their language may illuminate the workings of his imagination.

It is difficult to go beyond this without sinking into unhelpful generality. Shakespeare supremely had the ability to speak for people far different from himself—the capacity that Keats identified as 'negative capability' that 'takes as much delight in conceiving an Iago as an Imogen',[2] as we see from the vast range of characters in his plays. If he could compose the anguished speeches of, say, Angelo, in *Measure for Measure*, or of Hamlet or Othello in their most passionate moments, if within a single scene he could express totally conflicting points of view, as he does in the Duke's consolation for death (3.1.5–31) and Claudio's passionate expression of fear of death (3.1.118–32) in *Measure for Measure*, he could also have written poems expressing points of view that he did not personally feel.

But though we may not ascribe sentiments expressed in the Sonnets to Shakespeare himself, we can at least say that the fact that he expressed them indicates a capacity within himself to think such thoughts even if he does not identify with them. On that basis we may say, for what it is worth, that he understood the feelings of those who succeed in love, and those who fail; that he understood the pain of physical separation from the beloved and of emotional estrangement; that he could enter into the imaginations of men who felt deep love and desire for individual men and women; and that he knew what it was to be profoundly, even self-destructively introspective. The Sonnets do not necessarily have to entertain, advise, or inform other readers, but may rather show the poet struggling to understand himself. In this sense they may be thought of as an emotional autobiography.

In the chapters that follow we shall explore the techniques and results of Shakespeare's literary self-examination.

The Form of Shakespeare's Sonnets

In this chapter we shall discuss the overall form as it relates to the arrangement of the collection and its subsections. We consider formal characteristics of individual poems in Chapter 5.

We have said that the poems are more properly regarded as a collection than as a sequence. They do not hang together on the thread of a single narrative or by virtue of a single addressee. Almost all of them are love poems in the sense that they address a loved person or spring out of the poet's shifting relationship with such a person, and changes in the relationships hint at an underlying narrative, but it can scarcely be called a story.

As the collection was first printed it falls into two major divisions. The first 126 poems include none that are clearly addressed to, or concern, a woman, along with all the ones that are clearly addressed to, or primarily concern, a male. The sonnets from 127 onwards include all the poems that are overtly addressed to, or primarily concern, a female. This is clearly a deliberate and careful division. But it should not be assumed that the first part does not include any poems which might be addressed to a woman, and vice versa. As Colin Burrow writes, in these poems 'one is not quite sure who is male and who is female, who is addressed or why, or what their respective social roles are' (p. 91). Nor should it be taken for granted that all the poems in the first part refer to a man, however likely this may seem. Some of the poems in the first part are regularly reprinted in anthologies as non-specific love poems. In particular, Sonnet 18, 'Shall I compare thee to a summer's day?', is often taken to refer to a woman, and Sonnet 116, 'Let me not to the marriage of true minds', is a popular choice for reading at heterosexual weddings and funerals. Table 1 shows more clearly how the collection can be gendered, depending on questions of context and ordering.

The last poem of the first group, beginning 'O thou, my lovely boy', is not a strict sonnet, being a series of six rhyming pentameter couplets, as if the sonnet were entirely made up of conclusions. There are then only twelve lines in the poem in which the poet relinquishes the power of his love to the inevitability of Time. Because of its placing and its formal irregularity this poem is sometimes described as an envoi—a farewell, or closing poem. It marks a clear end to the first major part of the collection. In the 1609 Quarto two open, line-long empty brackets paradoxically emphasize the absence of lines 13 and 14, suggesting perhaps that they have been erased by Time making 'Her audit (though delayed)'—presumably over 125 sonnets.

Though the poem has something of the typical sonnet structure (discussed in Chapter 5, below), in its original printing it is followed enigmatically by two pairs of brackets. Although for many years the general assumption was that the parentheses were simply a printer's aberration, or his way of indicating that the poem appeared to be incomplete, more recently they have been relentlessly interrogated,

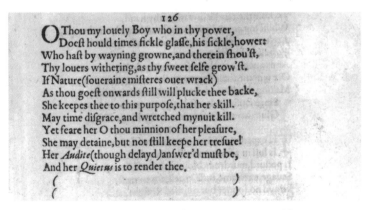

Fig. 6. The empty brackets printed after the twelve lines of Sonnet 126 have provoked much speculation about their significance.

Table 1. *Sexing the Sonnets: Male and Female addressees*
Sonnets which suggest a male addressee

1	33
3	39
6	41
7	42
9	63
13	67
16	68
19	101
20	108
26	126

Sonnets which might imply a male addressee, either because of their context, or because of their subject matter, but which could imply either a male or a female, if read independently

2	36
4	54
5	79
8	80
10	81
11	82
12	83
14	84
15	85
34	86
35	

Sonnets which suggest a female addressee

127	141
130	145
138	151
139	

Sonnets which might imply a female addressee, either because of their context, or because of their subject matter, but which could imply either a male or a female, if read independently

93	134
119	135
131	136
132	147
133	152

Sonnets which refer to male and female subjects

41	106
53	144

yielding an extraordinary range of interpretations which must derive rather from the reader than from the author. They have been compared to the (empty) marks in an account book; to the shape of an hourglass that contains no sand; to little moons that 'image a repeated waxing and waning of the moon, pointing to fickleness and frailty' (quoted in Duncan-Jones, p. 126); to representations of a grave; and—because they stand in for a couplet—to the image of a failure to couple. They may be seen as marking a breathing space before the reader embarks on the second part; in their suggestion of curtailment they may indicate that the male/male relationship of the first part has petered out in insterility; they may even invite readers to contribute a couplet of their own devising.

By our count, only twenty of the poems, all in the first group (Sonnets 1–126), can confidently be said, on the evidence of forms of address and masculine pronouns, to be addressed to, or to concern, a male, while seven, all in the second group (Sonnets 127–52), are clearly about a female. Other sonnets which might seem definite about the gender of their addressees rely on context, or subject matter, rather than pronouns (see Table 1). As we shall see, some of the poems in the earlier group relate to the poet's relationship with a woman, and four of those in the later part—Nos. 133, 134, 135, and 144—show the poet anguishing about his relationship between a man and a woman; in the last of these, Sonnet 144—'Two loves I have, of comfort and despair'— he is torn between a man and a woman, and pretty clearly prefers the man, his 'better angel'. All the rest of the poems in the collection (those not listed individually on Table 1) could in theory be addressed to, or be about, either a male or a female. Some of the most intense love poems, such as Sonnets 27, 43, and 61, could, considered on their own, be addressed either to a male or to a female.

Of the 154 poems in the collection, 123 are addressed to an individual, whether male or female. The remaining thirty-one vary in their degree of relevance and connection to those that surround them. So, for example, Sonnet 5 when considered on its own is a meditation on the effects of time on human and natural beauty, concluding with the reflection that they can be countered by 'distillation' (l. 9). But it leads straight into the following poem which, beginning 'Then let not . . .', applies to an individual the moral implied in the preceding one. The structure of the two poems taken together resembles that of Sonnet 12, where a generalized reflection on the effects of time is applied to an individual; in Sonnets 5 and 6, however, the generalization takes up one sonnet and its application another. These poems form a double sonnet which is essentially a single poem. Others are linked through contradiction (for example, Nos. 73 and 74). Some sonnets without personal addressees are linked to their neighbours in that, though they do not address anyone in particular, they write about a specific individual in the third person, for example Nos. 63–8—a mini-sequence in the first three of which the poet reflects upon the effects of time on his love, followed by three in which world-weariness is redeemed only by thought of the beloved. Other short sequences within the collection are linked by theme or subject matter, for example Nos. 100–3, in which the poet is searching for and responding to his muse. Many small groupings may be suggested within the collection as a whole; more are listed in Table 2.

Three poems have no obvious thematic connections with the sequence and could have been printed independently as generalized meditations. First is Sonnet 94, the enigmatic 'They that have power to hurt and will do none...', which in subject matter seems out of place in a collection of love poems (though the imagery of flowers in its sestet looks forward to the sonnet that follows). It comes in the midst of a sequence of loosely connected poems, stretching back at least as far as Sonnet 79, in which initially the poet expresses jealousy of a rival poet. There is nothing in any of the 'rival poet' poems to show that they are addressed to a male; the assumption that they are derives from the fact that they are in the first part of the collection and from their link with the love triangle revealed in Sonnets 133–6 and 144. Increasingly the poet resents the beloved's love of praise, regretting his own incapacity to supply it. Sonnet 87 is a poem of renunciation—'Farewell, thou art too dear for my possessing' (l. 1)—and in the following three the still-loving poet declares himself not merely guilty of any faults that his lover may find in him but willing to take disgrace upon himself if it will help to justify his lover in joining with the rest of the world to spite him (Sonnet 90, l. 3). There is a little relief in Sonnet 91, where the relationship seems to have been partly resumed though it is still precarious: 'thou mayst take | All this away, and me most wretched make' (ll. 13–14). In Sonnet 92 he fears that the beloved may 'be false, and yet I know it not' (l. 14), and this

Table 2. *Groups of sonnets*

Note: Identifying groups of sonnets within the collection will always be, to some extent, subjectively inflected. This table has no claim to exhaustiveness in its search for links between one sonnet and another/others.

Small groups of sonnets and sequences within Shakespeare's collection	Reason for linkage: a *keyword*, or theme
1–17	Persuasion to procreate
5 and 6	*Then*
9 and 10	*shame* (last line of 9, first line of 10)
15, 16, and 17	Writing for eternity
23 and 24	Eyesight
27 and 28	Insomnia
33 and 34	Weather and relationship
40, 41 and 42	Attacking, love triangle
44 and 45	The four elements
46 and 47	*Eye* and *heart*
50 and 51	*Thus* and journey
55–60	Different experiences of Time when in love
57 and 58	Slave of love
63, 64, 65, 66, 67 and 68	Time and beauty
67 and 68	*Thus*
69 and 70	Blame
71 and 72	*World*
73 and 74	*But*
78, 79, 80, 82, 83, 84, 85 and 86	Rival poet/s
88, 89 and 90	*Against myself*, hate
91, 92 and 93	*But*, falsity
97, 98 and 99	Seasons
100, 101, 102, and 103	Muse sonnets (Muse also mentioned in others)
106, 107, 108, and 109	Echoes on writing, peace, and time (Kerrigan, pp. 8–9)
109 and 110	Contradiction of constancy and falsity
111 and 112	Pity
113 and 114	*Mind*
118 and 119	Sickness/Fever
125 and 126	*Render*
129 and 130	Stand alone sonnets, work almost antithetically, unusual so close together
131, 132 and 133	Groaning sonnets
131, 132, 133, 134, 135, and 136	Love triangle
134, 135, and 136	*Will*
140, 141, and 142	*Eyes* and *sin*
(137), 138, 139, 140, 141, and 142	Lies, dishonesty
153 and 154	Classical allusions, Cupid, translations

leads into Sonnet 93 in which he imagines himself 'like a deceivèd husband' (l. 2). (This is the only phrase in the whole mini-sequence which might be taken to imply that the poet is addressing a male; he could not feel *like* a husband if he were addressing his wife, and it would seem odd to use this phrase of a mistress.) This poem anticipates Sonnet 138, which is clearly about a woman, in its willingness to accept false appearances as reality. The idea that the beloved's beauty is such that, 'whate'er thy thoughts or thy heart's workings be, | Thy looks should nothing thence but sweetness tell' (Sonnet 93, ll. 11–12) provides at least a hint of a context for the otherwise independent Sonnet 94, which is about people who are 'lords and owners of their faces' (l. 7). It's not, however, the same—in Sonnet 93 the person addressed simply cannot express anything but 'sweetness' (l. 12), whereas in Sonnet 94 he or she has and exercises the ability to keep his or her features under complete control. But perhaps it's enough to plant a seed from which Sonnet 94 may have sprung. It may also be relevant that the ability to control facial expression is a virtue in members of the acting profession to which Shakespeare belonged.

The enigma in this poem resides partly in these lines:

> The summer's flower is to the summer sweet,
> Though to itself it only live and die,
> But if that flower with base infection meet,
> The basest weed outbraves his dignity:
>> For sweetest things turn sourest by their deeds;
>> Lilies that fester smell far worse than weeds.
>
> (Sonnet 94, ll. 9–14)

What exactly is it saying? The first two lines refer to people who restrain themselves from causing hurt even if they 'show' the desire to do so. The next two indicate, however, that these people remain impassive even while 'moving others'—to what? Then we are told that these people 'rightly do inherit nature's graces', as if the qualities we have been told they display deserve reward, which is not entirely evident. Lines 7 and 8 seem as if they should sum up what has so far been said: 'They are the lords and owners of their faces, | Others but stewards of their excellence.' Is impassivity a virtue? In what sense are people who cannot control their expressions 'stewards of their excellence'? Are they stewards of their own excellence, or of the excellence of those who are 'lords and owners of their faces'?

The rest of the sonnet is more straightforward. Metaphorically it says that beauty ('the summer's flower') is sweet even if it does not propagate itself ('Though to itself it only live and die'), but if it becomes infected it is worth no more than 'The basest weed'. What is the tenor of the metaphor? And the couplet appears to be trying to make a link with the octave: 'For sweetest things turn sourest by their deeds. | Lilies that fester smell far worse than weeds'. (This last line is found also in the anonymous play, attributed at least in part to Shakespeare, *Edward III*. Though proverbial in tone, it has not been found elsewhere.) But what exactly is the link? The poem struggles to give an impression of profundity but its excessive use of generalization and metaphor inhibits communication.

The next poem that lacks clear links to its companions, though it is relevant enough as a withdrawal from the particular to the general in a love sequence, is Sonnet 116, 'Let me not to the marriage of true minds', an eloquent tribute to the power of love which nevertheless has a sting in its tail: 'If this be error and upon me proved, | I never writ, nor no man ever loved' (ll. 13–14). Does this mean that it is not an error, or that it is an illusion to which all lovers are susceptible? And, for that matter, do the last words stand independently as 'no man ever loved' or refer back to 'I' to mean 'I never loved any man'? And is the poem a tribute to the power of love in general, or of love of man to woman (as generally supposed) or of man for man, as the context might suggest?

Most detached of all is the great but damaged Sonnet 146, which would be more at home in a religious than in an amatory sequence. It may be significant that it immediately follows the Anne Hathaway sonnet (No. 145), which also seems irrelevantly imported into the collection. The antithesis between soul and body has occurred earlier, and will be repeated in a grosser context in Sonnet 151 (see pp. 53, 71, below). It is a Renaissance topos; *Love's Labour's Lost* might be regarded as an extended dramatization of it. Shakespeare develops it here with consummate skill in a perfectly formed poem, marred only by the textual dislocation in its second line. The couplet is worthy of

John Donne ('Death, thou shalt die', *Holy Sonnets*, 6) and anticipates
Dylan Thomas's 'Death, thou shalt have no dominion' (itself biblical
in origin): addressing his soul, Shakespeare writes

> So shalt thou feed on Death, that feeds on men,
> And Death once dead, there's no more dying then.
>
> (Sonnet 146, ll. 13–14)

The Chronology of the Collection

Discussion of the form of the collection cannot avoid consideration of
whether it was written as a whole, and if not, when individual poems
were composed. This is a highly contentious topic. Although
the Sonnets were not initially written in the order in which they are
printed in the 1609 text, there are a few fixed points. As we have seen
(pp. 22–3), the irregular Sonnet 145, with its puns on Hathaway, is
probably the earliest, dating from around 1581–2. Francis Meres's
reference to Shakespeare's 'sugared sonnets' in 1598 shows that some
of them were written by then (curiously, the phrase 'sugared sonnets'
also occurs in Barnfield's *Greene's Funerals*, of 1594: Sonnet 9—a
poem in the six-line stanza form of *Venus and Adonis*—l. 15. Meres
declares himself a friend of Barnfield, who as we have seen was a fan of
both Marlowe and Shakespeare; it looks if they may have formed
something of a poetic circle). There is no absolute certainty that these
sonnets are among those printed in 1609; and 'sonnets' could mean
simply lyrics. But in 1599 versions of two sonnets, Nos. 138 ('When my
love swears that she is made of truth') and 144 ('Two loves I have,
of comfort and despair'), appear as Shakespeare's in *The Passionate
Pilgrim*. As this is an unauthorized publication (see pp. 3–4) we must
suppose that they were printed from a privately circulated manuscript,
presumably released by an indiscreet 'private friend'. Both are among
Shakespeare's more intimate poems; maybe this, as much as the fact
that they were printed without authority, was what caused Shakespeare's sense of offence with the publisher. And both, obviously, were
finally printed in the later part of the collection. The latest datable
sonnet may be No. 107, in which the line 'The mortal moon hath her
eclipse endured' may, but does not certainly, refer obliquely to the
death of Queen Elizabeth in 1603.

The poems may then have been written over a period of some twenty years, and some could even date from as late as the year in which the collection first appeared; this is in itself an argument against the supposition, once current, that they were conceived as a sequence. Beyond this, attempts to date them have to rely principally on evidence from literary context and style, neither of which is infallible. The vogue for sonnet sequences initiated by the publication of Sidney's *Astrophil and Stella* in 1591 climaxed around 1596. Shakespeare's use of the form in plays extends, as we shall see in Chapter 7, as far as *Cymbeline*, written about 1610, but is most apparent in *Love's Labour's Lost* and *Romeo and Juliet*, of around 1595. This is in any case the period during which Shakespeare makes most use of lyric forms in his plays—*A Midsummer Night's Dream* is another example—so it would not be surprising to find him writing sonnets at the same time. Readers who know Shakespeare's plays may easily be tempted to see a broad resemblance between the stylistic development apparent in them and that between the earliest and latest printed poems in the collection. Shakespeare's earliest plays are those that display the greatest formality of style. The first seventeen of the Sonnets, which all play variations on the theme of procreation and are relatively distanced in their use of the sonnet form, may seem to belong to the same world as the early comedies.

The later sonnets include some of the most intense poems, resembling some of the anguished self-revelations of characters in the plays. The common impression that the latest printed poems were also the last to be written is based on a subjective reaction—not necessarily any the worse for that, but in contradiction to the results of recent, more scientifically based studies. Some of these rely on analyses of the Sonnets' vocabulary in relation to that of the plays (whose chronology itself is also, it has to be admitted, far from certain). They identify words that occur rarely within the canon as a whole, and within plays that are close in date of composition. Occurrence of such words within the Sonnets is taken to indicate composition around the same date. Studies carried out by MacDonald P. Jackson suggest that most of the sonnets from Nos. 1 to 103, and 127 to the end, were written from 1593 to 1599 (when the vogue for the sonnet form was at its height), that most of the so-called 'Dark Lady' sonnets are among the earliest, and that most of the sonnets from Nos. 104 to 126 were written in the seventeenth century. Jackson believes it is unhelpful to think of the Sonnets as chronologically homogeneous and that Burrow's edition (p. 105) represents the dating of the Sonnets too tidily. Burrow suggests, for example, that the latest sonnets were finished by 1604. We believe that, on balance, there can be no immediate objection to the proposition that Shakespeare was still writing or revising Sonnets up until their publication in 1609.[1] The fairly recent theory that the differences between Nos. 138 and 144 as printed first in *The Passionate Pilgrim* in 1599 and later in 1609 result from revision rather than corruption in the earlier publication encourages the idea that individual sonnets may have been subject to some degree of revision at the time that they were assembled as a collection, presumably by Shakespeare himself. Other poets did the same kind of thing: Michael Drayton, for instance, reworked his sequence, first published as *Idea* in 1594, over a period of twenty years until it appeared in its final form as *Idea's Mirror* in 1619. It seems clear, then, that at some point in the early seventeenth century someone, presumably Shakespeare himself, arranged a pre-existing set of poems in which smaller groupings exist and in which connections concerned with dates of composition can be identified.

Within the two major divisions a number of other groupings may be discerned. Most clearly, the first seventeen poems as printed include all those that implore a young man to marry and to have children. Another mini-sequence of poems about separation and absence preluded by Sonnet 39—'let us divided live' (l. 5)—is taken up by Sonnets 41 and 42 in which it is linked with the theme of the youth's infidelity with the poet's mistress, and continues to Sonnet 52—'So am I as the rich...'. It is interrupted by the nevertheless not-unrelated Sonnet 49, in which the poet meditates on how he might feel if the youth deserted him. Within this subgroup come pairs of sonnets which together virtually constitute a single poem. Sonnet 44's concern with two of the elements, earth and water, is picked up in the first line of Sonnet 45, 'The other two, slight air and purging fire'. Then Sonnet 46, beginning 'Mine eye and heart are at a mortal war', is followed by one beginning 'Betwixt mine eye and heart a league is took'. As we have said (p. 26), Nos. 79 to 80 and 83 to 86 concern the poet's rivalry with another poet for the young man's favours; the preceding sonnet—No. 78—may be regarded as a prelude since in it the poet writes of how 'every alien pen' (l. 3) has found inspiration in his friend's beauty.

Some of the links between sonnets discussed above may result from contiguity of composition. Indeed certain linked sonnets may also be regarded as 'double sonnets', or two-part poems. Other links may be the result rather of reorganization after the initial act of composition. It is often argued that the placing of certain sonnets has numerological significance. The numbering of Sonnet 60, with its emphasis on minutes and hours, is clearly appropriate. And the number 12 fits well with the ticking rhythm of that sonnet's opening line—'When I do count the clock that tells the time'. The physical effects of time on the lover are discussed in both Sonnet 63, the age at which the human body was thought to face its major crisis in development, or 'grand climacteric', and Sonnet 49, the age at which a 'minor climacteric' was believed to occur. It is difficult to know whether to ascribe esoteric significance to the matches between number and content or to put them down to coincidence. They may be no more than a sophisticated kind of game with the reader, or a way of adding a few grace notes by way of decoration. If they are intentional the numbering must be Shakespeare's own, which might otherwise be doubted: the poems may have been unnumbered in the manuscript, and numbers may have been added either by a scribe or by a compositor.

Beliefs about the date of the Sonnets have critical consequences. As we have seen, the possibility that they were written over a long period of time, as well as the fact that they are not necessarily printed in the order in which they were composed, is a reason for questioning whether there may have been more than one friend, more than one lover. So, if the Sonnets are 'about' specific individuals, possibly commissioned or presented as gifts to Shakespeare's 'private friends', there may have been more than two of them. At least four kinds of persons, three males and one female, figure in the collection. One is the poetic voice (and this may be reimagined as female); another is a male addressee. A third is a poet who is amorously entangled with both a male addressee and the fourth person, a 'black' woman who is the initial poet's lover. Various characteristics which could be attributed to these personae may be identified, and an attempt to do this may help to illuminate a particular dimension of the sequence. The shifting impressionism of the poems' characterization creates a desire for a precision which the poems themselves deny. So we must emphasize that since the addressees may not remain constant throughout the collection, these characteristics may not inhere in any single individual, whether real or imaginary.

The Poet's Voice

The poet—or perhaps we should say the shifting persona of the poet—reveals a few aspects of himself relevant to the implied narrative at different points in the collection. The poet never states that he is married; he even goes so far as to suggest that his relationship to the male friend resembles that of a wife to her husband: 'So shall I live, supposing thou art true, | Like a deceivèd husband' (No. 93, ll. 1–2). He has, however, a female partner, not only in the second but also in the first part; Sonnet 41, for instance, rebukes the friend for breaking a 'two-fold troth: | Hers, by thy beauty tempting her to thee, | Thine, by thy beauty being false to me' (ll. 12–14). In some of the poems the poet is older than the friend, most obviously in Sonnet 73:

> That time of year thou mayst in me behold
> When yellow leaves, or none, or few do hang
> Upon those boughs which shake against the cold,
> Bare ruined choirs, where late the sweet birds sang.
>
> (ll. 1–4)

In Sonnet 62 he describes himself as 'Beated and chapped with tanned antiquity' (l. 10), and in Sonnet 138 says that his mistress 'knows [his] days are past the best' (l. 6). Though some of the poet's expressions of unworthiness ('Being your slave . . .', No. 57, l. 1) may simply be poetic tropes, at various points he expresses a sense of being victimized: 'Now, while the world is bent my deeds to cross, | Join with the spite of Fortune' (No. 90, ll. 2–3), 'O, for my sake do you with Fortune chide, | The guilty goddess of my harmful deeds' (No. 111, ll. 1–2). He is the victim of an unspecified 'vulgar scandal' (No. 112, ll. 2). A sense of his own unworthiness in comparison with the beloved is a recurrent theme. Some unspecified cause, a 'separable spite' (No. 36, ll. 6), often keeps him apart from his friend—is this disparity of rank?—

geographical separation?—the poet's married state?—the fact that they are both male?; a number of the Sonnets express grief and longing in absence. He loves both the friend and a woman who is 'black' in appearance and in character, and is torn between them. As we have seen (p. 24), the poet's name is Will[iam] (Nos. 135–6, and possibly No. 143).

The Young Man (or Men)

A beloved is not certainly named, though it is possible to infer from the puns throughout Sonnets 135 and 136 that he too is a Will. He is certainly unmarried in some of the poems, and none of the others contradicts this. Early poems in the collection address a man in loving terms while criticizing, sometimes harshly, his selfishness in failing to marry and so to defy time by passing his beauty on to posterity.

One feature of Shakespeare's collection that differentiates it from all others is that the beloved, though frequently idealized in the first part, is nevertheless faulty: 'for the first time in the entire history of the sonnet, the desired object is *flawed*' (Spiller, p. 156). This is true of both parts of the collection. Sonnet 35—and, in conjunction with it, the preceding two poems—alludes to an unnamed 'trespass' (l. 6), a 'sensual fault' (l. 9) which the poet forgives; Sonnet 41 speaks of 'pretty wrongs that liberty commits' (l. 1) and clearly implies that the friend has offended sexually with the poet's mistress:

> yet thou mightst my seat forbear,
> And chide thy beauty and thy straying youth,
> Who lead thee in their riot even there
> Where thou art forced to break a two-fold truth:
> Hers, by thy beauty tempting her to thee,
> Thine, by thy beauty being false to me.
>
> (ll. 9–14)

The poem that follows (No. 42) says that, though the poet loved the woman dearly, 'That she hath thee is of my wailing chief, | A loss in love that toucheth me more nearly' (ll. 3–4). Yet in a later, or at least later numbered, poem (Sonnet 53) the poet can write of his beloved's 'constant heart' (l. 14). In Sonnet 67 a young man is apparently accused of keeping bad company. Sonnet 70 defends him against unspecified slander to his 'pure unstained prime' (l. 8). Sonnets 78–80 and 81–6 are those concerned with the 'rival poets' (see below). There is an implication in the couplet of Sonnet 88 that the poet is willing to take responsibility for his friend's wrongs (it is not clear whether the 'faults concealed' of line 7 are the friend's as well as the poet's), and this poem is followed by others such as Sonnets 93, 95–6, and 120 which show a troubled sense of the friend's transgressions.

In spite of his rebukes, the poet, as in sonnet sequences of the period addressed to women, shows a determination to idealize the beloved. We shall say more about the qualities ascribed to the friend and the emotional states that he provokes in writing about the content of the Sonnets (Chapter 6).

A Woman—or Some Women

As we have seen, it is common in sonnet sequences of the period for the woman addressed to bear a romantic, often classically derived name—Laura, Diella, Celia, Idea, Diana, Zepheria, and so on. No woman's name, whether romantic or ordinary, attaches itself to the woman (or women) of Shakespeare's sonnets. She is spoken of or addressed only generically as, for instance, 'my mistress' (Nos. 127. l. 9; 130, l. 13), 'my music' (No. 128, l. 1, not specifically addressed to a woman), 'my love' (No. 130, l. 13), and 'Dear heart' (No. 139, l. 6). The term 'dark lady', which in popular and even in critical usage has attached itself to the Sonnets, is an imposition upon them. 'Lady' is not found, and 'dark' only once (No. 147, l. 14). Even 'black' occurs in only five of the sonnets (Nos. 127, 130, 131, 132, and 147). In three of them it is the occasion for praise: the woman's (natural) blackness of eyes and brows shames those who make fair 'the foul with art's false borrowed face' (Nos. 127, l. 6); though (parodically) 'black wires grow on her head' yet the lover thinks her 'rare | As any she belied with false compare' (No. 130, ll. 4, 14). Her black eyes demonstrate her mourning for his 'pain'; and if her heart would mourn for his too, he would 'swear beauty herself is black, | And all they foul that thy complexion lack' (No. 132, ll. 4, 13–14). In two of the poems, however, 'black' provides an occasion for bitter wordplay on the word's literal and metaphorical senses. 'Thinking on' her 'face' he regards her 'black' as 'fair', but she is 'black' in her 'deeds' (No. 131, ll. 10–13). His 'thoughts' and 'discourse' are 'as madmen's are' because he has 'sworn thee fair, and thought thee bright, | Who art as black as hell, and dark as night' (No. 147, ll. 11, 13–14). In Sonnet 152, though she is not explicitly 'black', the poet has falsely 'sworn [her] fair' (l. 13), and in Sonnet 144 she is 'coloured ill' (l. 4).

There are, then, only seven among the second group of twenty-eight sonnets in which a woman is explicitly or implicitly dark in colouring. There are, however, other poems in which a woman whom the poet loves is reviled as dark in character. Although Sonnet 129—'Th'expense of spirit in a waste of shame'—could, considered on its own, be unrelated to the rest of the collection, in context it reads like a poem of self-condemnation for the poet's subjugation to sexual desire. The difficult Sonnet 133 curses 'that heart that makes my heart to groan | For that deep wound it gives my friend and me' (ll. 1–2). Not only has the woman betrayed the poet, she has also enslaved his 'sweet'st friend', his 'next self', so that 'Of him, myself, and thee I am forsaken'. Nothing is left: he is bereft of himself, of the 'sweet'st friend' who is his 'next self', and of the woman herself. His heart is imprisoned in her 'steel bosom'; he pleads that she will at least let his own heart stand bail for his friend's so that he can be the friend's prison-warder. The friend means even more to him than the woman.

Sonnet 134 runs straight on to beg the 'covetous' woman to restore his 'kind' friend to him. But there is no hope: 'Him have I lost; thou hast both him and me; | He pays the whole, and yet am I not free' (ll. 13–14). Then, in Sonnet 135, he puns tortuously and despairingly on the word 'will'. The word occurs thirteen times in this sonnet; on seven of these occurrences in the Quarto it is both italicized and capitalized; the same is true of three of its seven occurrences in No. 136 and of its single one in No. 143, where again a pun is clearly intended. Although such details could derive from the compositor, some at least of these are likely to have been marked in the manuscript.

So many senses of the word are pertinent in Sonnet 135 that it is often difficult to say which is uppermost, or even whether particular ones are present at any given point. Of course they may be present in the reader's mind even if they were not in the poet's. And we cannot be sure at what points capitalization should be used in a modern text to indicate the personal name. In the opening lines the name seems to be dominant: 'Whoever hath her wish, thou hast thy will, | And Will to boot, and Will in overplus'—that is, Will (the poet) is subjugated to her will (in the primary sense of sexual desire). The idea that she has 'will' in overplus may, in view of the following line—'More than enough am I that vex thee still'—act simply as an apology for continuing to trouble her, but could also imply that she is oversexed, and must surely also suggest that this is the name of his friend. If this is agreed it strengthens the case for a real-life addressee. In the following lines 'will' in the senses successively of vagina and penis dominates:

> Wilt thou, whose will is large and spacious,
> Not once vouchsafe to hide my will in thine?
> Shall will in others seem right gracious,
> And in my will no fair acceptance shine?

(ll. 5–8)

Then in the sestet multiple meanings proliferate: 'So thou, being rich in will'—that is, in sexuality, and the organs of the lovers named

136

IF thy foule check thee that I come fo neere,
Sweare to thy blind foule that I was thy *Will*,
And will thy foule knowes is admitted there,
Thus farre for loue, my loue-fute fweet **fullfill.**
Will, will fulfill the treafure of thy lou**e,**
I fill it full with wils, and my will one,
In things of great receit with eafe we prooue,
Among a number one is reckon'd none.
Then in the number let me paffe vntold,
Though in thy ftores account I one muft be,
For nothing hold me, fo it pleafe thee hold,
That nothing me, a fome-thing fweet to thee.
   Make but my name thy loue, and loue that ftill,
   And then thou loueft me for my name is *Will.*

Fig. 7. Printers in Shakespeare's time felt free to alter details of the way texts were presented in their manuscripts, including capitalization and italicization; and the manuscript used for the Sonnets may not have been in Shakespeare's hand. Nevertheless, it is difficult not to attribute significance to the use of italics and capitals for seven of the thirteen instances of the word 'will' in Sonnet 135; Sonnet 136 (above) ends with the words 'my name is *Will.*'

Will—'add to thy Will | One will of mine to make thy large Will more' (ll. 11–12)—that is, if she agrees to his demands she will increase her sexual appetite (with a possible, however improbable, secondary sense of 'enlarge her vagina by enclosing his penis in it along with all the others'). Sonnet 152 implies not simply infidelity but adultery in that she has broken her 'bed-vow' (l. 3)—in other words, that she is married.

Other Poets

Along with the poet, the male friend (or friends), and the woman (or women) of the second group of sonnets, there is at least one additional though shadowy player in the drama, often known as 'the rival poet'. (While context suggests that the relevant poems—Sonnets 78–86—are about male friends, as is always assumed, it has to be admitted that so far as their content goes they could be addressed to a woman. Likewise, depending on how the Sonnets are spoken or the context in which they are reproduced, some could be imagined as being from a female to a female.) In Sonnet 79 the poet complains that his 'sick Muse' has had to give way to another (l. 4), and plays with the conceit that his rival's praise is worthless because all the qualities he (the rival) ascribes to the friend were there already. Sonnet 80 sees the poet panicking because a 'better spirit' (l. 2) is praising his friend, Sonnet 83 refers to 'both your poets' (l. 14; as Burrow says, this 'presumably refers to Shakespeare plus the rival, but it could conceivably refer to two rivals'); Sonnet 84 has a conceit similar to that of Sonnet 79 while rebuking the friend for being 'fond on praise' (l. 14), in Sonnet 85 the poet claims to be 'tongue-tied' (l. 1) in face of the rival's praise, while asking the friend to respect him for his 'dumb thoughts' (l. 14), and Sonnet 86 again expresses humility in face of the 'proud full sail' of the rival's 'great verse' (l. 1).

Little more can be deduced about this poet. He appears to be regarded as learned: the friend's eyes have 'added feathers to the learned's wing' (No. 78, l. 7); the friend is 'all my art, and dost advance | As high as learning my rude ignorance' (No. 78, ll. 13–14), and Sonnet 86 speaks mysteriously of 'his spirit, by spirits taught to write | Above a mortal pitch', of 'his compeers by night | Giving him aid', and of

'that affable familiar ghost | Which nightly gulls him with intelligence'
(ll. 5–10).

There are then scattered gestures towards an impressionistic narrative that could lie behind the Sonnets. The poet loves one or more young men, and/or women, and his love is to some degree reciprocated. The poet also loves a 'black' woman. Another poet also loves the person or persons, who respond to his praise. One or more women has an affair with one or more young men which the poet deeply resents. There is no resolution to the situation.

The Sonnets conform to no predetermined formal structure. The collection is like a patchwork composed of separately woven pieces of cloth, some bigger than others, some of them restitched, rearranged from time to time and finally sewn together in a composition that has only a deceptive, though at times satisfying, unity. It is as if Shakespeare were providing us with all the ingredients necessary to make our own series of narratives about love. To insist on one story alone is to misread the Sonnets and to ignore their will to plurality, to promiscuity. To seek for a tidy pattern in these loosely connected poems is like trying to control or tidy the inevitable mess and freedom that love itself creates.

The Artistry of Shakespeare's Sonnets

The experience of reading a Shakespearian sonnet is like a momentary vision: a sonnet can take anything from forty-five seconds (if read quickly) to just over a minute (if read slowly) to read out loud and, spatially, all its words can coexist as a physical printed body, suspended by the reader's gaze. To read the sonnet a second time helps to bring some of the detail of that same vision into focus through Shakespeare's arrangement of words, ideas, and sounds. A third reading makes the sonnet begin to appear like a carefully painted canvas in miniature. Words and phrases can become like paint and brushstrokes as the reader/viewer is possibly reminded of a preceding sonnet-canvas, and invited to make visual and semantic connections in Shakespeare's gallery of 154 exhibits. The sonnet then becomes like a living and moving painted image, depicted against the background of its own inextricable verbal music. Shakespeare, who usually engages artistically with a live theatre audience, here makes the Sonnets themselves his living art. It is often exhausting to look at paintings, and exquisitely miniaturized proportions do not necessarily ease viewing. The intensity of the sonnet form, the compact nature of the language, and the condensation of ideas make it difficult thoroughly to read more than a few sonnets at a single sitting. An understanding of how Shakespeare uses rhetorical and formal structural techniques in his sonnets will both convey the artistry at work within them, and provide an overall sense of what might be called the grammar of Shakespearian sonnet construction.

Sonnet 76 is positioned almost halfway through Shakespeare's collection and provides a useful starting point to consider Shakespeare's methods of poetic variation as well as the effect his sonnets have on a reader:

> Why is my verse so barren of new pride,
> So far from variation or quick change?
> Why with the time do I not glance aside
> To new-found methods, and to compounds strange?
> Why write I still all one, ever the same,
> And keep invention in a noted weed,
> That every word doth almost tell my name,
> Showing their birth, and where they did proceed?
> O know, sweet love, I always write of you,
> And you and love are still my argument;
> So all my best is dressing old words new,
> Spending again what is already spent:
>   For as the sun is daily new and old,
>   So is my love, still telling what is told.

The conceit of this poem relies on its self-reflexive quality. Shakespeare lays bare the problems facing a writer of such a disciplined form and mentions the limitation of subject matter, since he is obsessed by only singing the praises of his love. The reader is taken on a miniature journey which raises questions not only about the nature of the author's poetic endeavour, but about the other 153 sonnets which surround this one. Although the author might imply that the utter regularity of the sonnet form makes 'variation or quick change' impossible, the reader already knows that his sonnets so far have displayed many literary devices and rhetorical manoeuvres. That is partly why the reader has (possibly) already read seventy-five of them and is about to start on the second half of the collection. More variations and surprises will ensue. Somehow the poetic voice has been able to make its 'noted weed', its usual clothing, or poetic practice, 'keep invention' and seem fresh. Little wonder that the sonnet then alludes to childbirth, a metaphor of artistic creativity used in many of the other sonnets. If the author does not 'glance aside' to other devices, he is encouraging the reader to do precisely that by relating Sonnet 76 generally to its neighbouring poems. Richly suggestive, too, is the relationship between Shakespeare and the authorial persona he adopts, a connection so powerful 'That every word doth almost tell my name' (Sonnet 76, l. 7). If literary practice carries within it a distinctive genetic blueprint, then Shakespeare's poetic voice claims that the artistry in his poems reveals a recognizable tone of voice throughout—but regrets it.

By questioning its own artistry and the degree to which it might be related to Shakespeare's autobiography, Sonnet 76 makes clear two major, inevitable poles of possibility that any reader of the Sonnets has to address. Both have an impact on how the poems are read. The first relates to how far the Sonnets may properly be considered as individual poems and how far they should be read as part of a cycle of loosely connected poems which Shakespeare specifically ordered. The second pole of possibility relates to how far the Sonnets are autobiographical expressions of Shakespeare's own desires and thoughts, and how far they represent a purely literary exercise, potentially disconnected from real or actual experience. (See Table 3.)

Most studies and editions will position themselves, to varying degrees, somewhere in relation to these two poles of possibility; so too will each reader. Successful sonnet criticism tends to take a judiciously moderate stance and allows readers to discover for themselves where along the two broad ranges of possibilities they might place the poems. The position will probably vary on each reading since the Sonnets have an elusive quality and a habit of slipping through any net with which a critic or reader might attempt to entrap them.

Answers to most questions that might be asked of the Sonnets can be usefully related to the two broad areas of critical positioning just outlined. 'Who is the "Dark Lady"?', 'Who is the young man?' and 'Is

Table 3

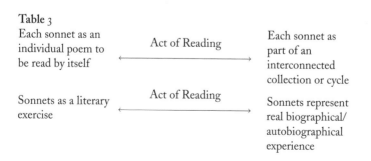

Each sonnet as an individual poem to be read by itself	Act of Reading ⟵—————⟶	Each sonnet as part of an interconnected collection or cycle
Sonnets as a literary exercise	Act of Reading ⟵—————⟶	Sonnets represent real biographical/ autobiographical experience

there more than one young man?', 'Did Shakespeare have a same-sex sexual relationship?', 'What story do the Sonnets tell?'—these are all questions which position the Sonnets as a sophisticated literary expression of Shakespeare's own personal and inner life. There is no straightforward way of answering any of them. To try to find supporting evidence from the Sonnets themselves is to select and discard, to break up the poems in illustration of an argument. Similarly, questions about the literary and cultural tradition of the Sonnets, the use Shakespeare is making of the poetic images and echoes of particular words and phrases might in the end ignore the integrity of individual poems. To emphasize this line of critical questioning does not focus sufficiently on the subjective interiority of the Sonnets, the intensely personal, intensely vulnerable emotions which they articulate to such great effect. Whilst it is satisfying to emphasize the pursuit of love through the many subtle webs of interconnectedness, such an approach defers the focus of each sonnet's integrity, what Gerard Manley Hopkins might call 'the achieve of, the mastery of the thing' ('The Windhover', l. 8). And yet, to focus only on a single sonnet is like removing a bright particular star from its constellation.

This tension between a general sonnet collection and the immediate demands of each individual poem streams through all sonnet criticism and remains an important consideration when thinking about Shakespeare's artistry. Coupled with the compression and density of the poems themselves, the Sonnets can soon become the most difficult and complicated part of the Shakespearian canon to read and discuss. Indeed, Colin Burrow refers to the Sonnets as 'a fusion of voices' (p. 135), which produce a potentially frustrating 'systematic elusiveness' (p. 138). He argues convincingly that 'Shakespeare's Sonnets use the methods of repetition and reapproximation which are central to the sonnet sequence to powerful effect.' It is as if the collection seems 'sourced in itself, and to be made up of readings and rereadings of its own poems' (p. 116). In this context, they can seem like a series of intense and related dramatic soliloquies or monologues which open up a richly mapped landscape of sound and sense. If this way of reading seems attractive, then on the two spectra of possibilities the act of reading might begin with the Sonnets as individual poems, but then move along the continuum towards the Sonnets being read as a whole collection of poems. On the other spectrum of possibility, the act of reading outlined would be positioned closest to the Sonnets as a literary exercise and away from any autobiographical interpretation.

Sonnet 76 serves as a challenging focus for artistic renegotiation within the collection of sonnets. It invites the reader to reconsider their relationship to the artist and addressee, or implied lover, at the same time. The propositions of Sonnet 76 are further complicated by the direct form of address, 'you', creating the artistic illusion that the sonnet intends a less intimate reader than a 'thou' as its lover. Since history obscures any sense of whether or not there was a real-life addressee for this particular sonnet, let alone the entire collection, to Sonnet 76 can be attributed a universal quality, which draws *any* of its potential readers into its own artistic world of creation, self-doubt, and paradoxically inspiring compromise: 'Spending again what is already spent' (l. 12). Moreover, like most of its 153 counterparts Sonnet 76 also empowers the reader to turn it into an act of performance by reading it to their own lover. So, the web of possibility is at least threefold. Sonnet 76 questions its context and emphasizes the tension between the general and the particular, it asks who is speaking to whom (Shakespeare to a lover or any reader; Shakespeare's imagined persona to an imagined lover or any reader), and it opens up ways in which it might be used as a poem by its readers in their own real or imagined lives. Sonnet 76 thus illustrates the power of all Shakespeare's sonnets to lead the reader into an imagined world of intimacy and readership, of desire and self-reflection.

The necessary practical and theoretical issues about the nature of the reading experience that the Sonnets permit, and its critical positioning, are inextricably related to Shakespeare's poetic power. The analogy of painting mentioned at the beginning of this chapter is utterly pertinent to an overall consideration of the sonnet form. Since a sonnet resembles a rectangle of canvas, it is possible for the reader's eye to hold suspended words as shapes and shades within a single frame of reference and to consider the sonnet as a spatial, as well as a literary, experience. Helen Vendler's microscopic, close readings of individual sonnets (see also Chapter 9, below) reveal rich structural patterns of keywords and sometimes individual letters. For example, Vendler (p. 84) sees Sonnet 9 as a 'Fantasy on the Letter W'. Absorbed in the structural near-symmetry of the word 'widdow', she identifies a richly obsessive exploration of the shapes and styles of words as letter patterns, made more emphatic, she argues, in old spelling, and through the conventions of printing-house practice. For Vendler, the sonnet is 'a flurry of *w*'s, *u*'s, and *v*'s'.

More generally the painting analogy relates to the physical possibilities of poetic shape and particularly the principle of the so-called classical golden ratio, or golden mean. A mathematical expression present in architecture, painting, and throughout the natural world—the proportions of a snail's shell and the petals of a daisy—the golden mean can also be discerned within the artistry of the sonnet form. If an area is divided into two sections according to the ratio 1 : 1.6 (approximately), then the lesser of the two sections is in precisely the same ratio to the greater, as the greater is to the area of the whole. In landscape paintings the point of the horizon often divides up the canvas according to the golden ratio; in music it is the proportional difference between the tonic and dominant notes in the thirteen parts of the chromatic scale. The eye senses an instinctive rightness in the painted landscape or in the proportions of a room; the ear tries to make the tonic complete by listening for the dominant note above it. As whole numbers the golden ratio can be expressed as 8 : 5, a whole divided into thirteen parts and proportionally arranged. A sonnet adds one more line to allow for a final rhyming couplet, but the point of division still occurs approximately at the golden section $((14 \div 13) \times 8 = 8.6$, with 5.4 left over to equal 14).[1] The idea of the sonnet often turns after the octave (the first eight lines) and changes the direction for the reader in the sestet (the next six lines). This turn is known as the volta and it occurs at a particularly satisfying moment for the human mind, eye, and ear. Spatially, then, there might be thought to be an underlying, classical principle for the sonnet as a literary form. Here, the Shakespearian sonnet can exist in creative tension with its Petrarchan antecedents, an earlier tradition which lends itself more readily to 8 : 6 because of its abbaabba–cdecde rhyme scheme. The Shakespearian volta can often seem deliberately weak, his form providing a different scope of subtlety and argumentative development. Shakespeare's form of three quatrains and a couplet makes the golden mean less apparent, and perhaps best perceived as a point of tension and identification with an earlier tradition.

If one looks to Sonnet 76 as an example of how the transition of thought changes, then it is clear that after asking three questions over eight lines, the defiant answer, the volta, comes at approximately the point of the golden mean, when the octave turns into the sestet: 'O know, sweet love, I always write of you' (l. 9). There are many instances of how Shakespeare changes the direction of one of his sonnets at the approximate point of the golden mean. Sonnets 29, 62, and 151 provide good illustrations of this much-used technique. These sonnets turn on the beginning of the sestet, thus:

> Yet in these thoughts myself almost despising
> (Sonnet 29, l. 9).

The poet's voice then goes on to describe a moment of liberation and transformational joy that comes just at the point when all seems lost. The self-obsessed narcissism of Sonnet 62 turns at the moment when the poet's theoretical assumptions about his own beauty are contradicted by practice and an objective, physical revelation:

> But when my glass shows me myself indeed
> (l. 9).

The poet then goes on to realize that any sense of self-worth is not independently possible, but is permitted by the way in which the self is made beautiful by the beloved:

> 'Tis thee (my self) that for myself I praise,
> Painting my age with beauty of thy days.
> (ll. 13–14)

Sonnet 151 sets up a dialectic between 'love' and 'conscience', between the 'body' and the 'soul'. In lines 7–8, the soul 'doth tell my body that he may | Triumph in love', and the poet does so by having an erection:

> But, rising at thy name, doth point out thee.
> (l. 9)

Here the volta coincides with the stirring of physical desire as well as with the synthesis of the whole argument.

One of the most easily recognizable ways of a Shakespeare sonnet turning at the golden mean is his use of the 'When'/'Then' strategy. Shakespeare is fond of using either word at the beginnings of lines (for example, Sonnets 2 and 43), but occasionally he uses them powerfully to divide the octave from the sestet so that the volta relies on the consequential 'Then'. Sonnets 12 and 15 are the purest examples of this technique:

> When I do count the clock that tells the time
>
> •   •   •   •   •
>
> Then of thy beauty do I question make
>
> (Sonnet 12, ll. 1, 9)
>
> When I consider everything that grows
>
> •   •   •   •   •
>
> Then the conceit of this inconstant stay
>
> (Sonnet 15, ll. 1, 9)

Variations on this technique include Sonnets 43, 51, 90, 106, and most notably Sonnet 30. Here Shakespeare takes the reader through two 'Then' transitions from the initial 'When' proposition in line 1. The reader is made to experience the intensity of the poet's meditation on memory and sadness. This extends through the 'When'/'Then' structure over twelve lines made up of a single sentence. The volta is delayed until the last possible moment, the rhyming couplet:

> But if the while I think on thee (dear friend)
> All losses are restored, and sorrows end.
>
> (Sonnet 30, ll. 13–14)

Sonnet 30's variation of the 'When'/'Then' strategy obviously shows that the volta does not always occur at the beginning of the sestet and crucially illustrates another overarching superstructure which Shakespeare uses to shape his sonnets. If a sonnet cannot be readily divided into an octave and sestet, then that is because the rhyme scheme of a Shakespeare sonnet imposes the structure of three quatrains (abab cdcd efef) and a rhyming couplet (gg). The three quatrains may develop a series of ideas which are then concluded by the final couplet, for example in Sonnet 1. In the first quatrain, the poet begins by discussing the procreation of beauty which will ensure that the young and beautiful will replace the old, but live as a testament to them. In the second quatrain, the poet then laments that his lover is too narcissistic and self-consumed, which far from creating beauty cruelly blights the self-perpetuation of more. The third quatrain praises and relates the lover's status to the natural world whilst turning that same comparison in on itself with the accusation that the lover is like a rose which will never flower. By this point, the lover has become the personification of natural beauty wasted. The final couplet suggests a possible resolution to the problem and asks the lover to take pity on the world. If not, then the lover will be no better than a glutton, consuming all the beauty of the world and taking it no further than the grave.

Sometimes Shakespeare calls attention to his tripartite quatrain structure by repeating the same word at the beginning of each quatrain. Sonnets 49 and 64 provide obvious examples of this technique; Sonnets 57 (with 'Nor'), 65 (with 'O'), and 73 (with 'thou mayst in me behold' in line 1 and 'In me thou seest' in lines 5 and 9) show how this practice might be more subtly deployed. Sometimes the poet uses each quatrain to ask one or perhaps two questions. The first eight lines of Sonnet 146 form a series of questions of diminishing length: four lines, then two lines, then one-and-a-half lines, then half a line. This can make the quatrains seem detached from each other and, crucially, from the final couplet, for example Sonnet 67. In Sonnet 42, the three quatrains and the couplet seem especially locked into one inextricably dense and progressive argument which makes its final conceit in the volta couplet all the more impressive. The revelation of the poet's joy has been hardly won and also functions as a reward for the reader. The traditional love triangle is overcome by the friendship between the two rivals:

> But here's the joy; my friend and I are one.
> Sweet flattery! Then she loves but me alone.
>
> (Sonnet 42, ll. 13–14)

And yet, this couplet can also seem like a definite irresolution of the problem, almost as if the poet has convinced himself, but no one else, of the outcome. The great conclusion to Sonnet 116 provides another example of similar tone:

> If this be error and upon me proved,
> I never writ, nor no man ever loved.

If *what* be error, and how is it possible to prove the negative case? The poet *has* written, irrespective of the argument of Sonnet 116, and has, it would seem, been a lover of men, as well as a lover among them.

Shakespearian sonnet couplets, then, seem usually to provide a conclusion, but this itself can sometimes paradoxically heighten the sense
of uncertainty.

The degree to which a Shakespeare sonnet demands to be thought
of as three quatrains and a couplet varies, and reveals just how differently sensitive Shakespeare remains throughout his collection to the
nuances of structure. Sonnet 56 is at once three quatrains and a couplet
and a subtle adaptation of that form into an octave and a sestet. There
seem to be two main movements in the poet's thought. The first, the
octave, considers the appetite of the lover; the second, the sestet,
compares the absence of the lover to the ocean which not only
associates itself with the feelings of appetite, Orsino-like (*Twelfth
Night*, 2.4.96), digesting the shore and then moving away from it
when full, but also pushes forward into a seasonal comparison in the
last two lines. Here, Shakespeare's thought develops and stretches
over the sestet rather than over two groups of four and two lines (the
third quatrain and the rhyming couplet):

> Let this sad interim like the ocean be,
> Which parts the shore where two, contracted new,
> Come daily to the banks, that when they see
> Return of love, more blest may be the view;
>   Or call it winter, which being full of care,
>   Makes summer's welcome thrice more wished, more rare.
>
>   (Sonnet 56, ll. 9–14).

Sonnet 56 itself is like a wave of thought and can be considered as two
movements: a drawing in and a pulling back; a consideration of the
lover 'thy', 'thou' and then a descriptive illustration which casts
the 'Return of love' into a third-person narrative, moving away from
the particular of the second-person singular.

Generally, Shakespeare's inevitable rhyming couplet seals the
preceding twelve lines with an emphatic sense of conclusion and
hives each sonnet off from others in the collection. The rhyming
couplet also has the effect of clearing the way for a reader's mind to
experience the next sonnet in its own right. Sometimes the couplet is
connected to the last six lines as in Sonnet 56 (Sonnets 90, 119, 121, and
140 illustrate this tendency further). At its weakest, the rhyming
couplet can seem tacked onto the preceding twelve lines. Sonnets 6,

18, 92, 131, 132, and 147 (the last three signalling the lover as 'black') are just some examples. Sonnet 36 has the same rhyming couplet as Sonnet 96:

> But do not so; I love thee in such sort
> As thou being mine, mine is thy good report.
> (Sonnets 36 and 96, ll. 13–14)

The couplet works equally well in both cases, serving as a possible connection between the two and might emphasize the passage of time, or a progression in the collection. The repetition is also suggestive of an oversight on Shakespeare's part and hints that on at least one occasion he might have regarded the couplet as an abstract unit of sense, not only detached from the preceding twelve lines, but interchangeable. The couplet's usual function is finally to state the thesis of the sonnet, to give an overview of the progression of thought. Occasionally, too, the couplet itself provides the volta. Perhaps one of the most interesting examples of Shakespeare's use of the couplet is in Sonnet 34. Employing a directness of diction throughout in what seems like a lover's quarrel, the couplet implies that the lover/reader has begun to weep between the end of line 12 and the beginning of line 13:

> Th'offender's sorrow lends but weak relief
> To him that bears the strong offence's cross.
> Ah, but those tears are pearl which thy love sheds,
> And they are rich, and ransom all ill deeds.
> (Sonnet 34, ll. 11–14)

The effect is made even more powerful by the religious implications of 'cross', 'pearl', 'sheds' (like Christ's blood on the cross), and 'ransom', as well as 'wound', 'repent', and 'sorrow' earlier (ll. 8, 10, and 11).

Considering the Sonnets as a self-consciously ordered collection makes for many possible pathways of relationship between the openings and the final couplets. First of all the opening lines vary between the directly intimate in tone (for example, Sonnets 36, 67, 79, and 133) and the more public (for example, Sonnets 7, 24, 55, and 143). Sonnet 91 is followed in close relationship by Sonnet 92, but the former is public in its opening, 'Some glory in their birth, some in their skill', and the latter is intimate, 'But do thy worst to steal thyself away'. The sonnets often begin *in medias res* as though the reader is being taken immediately into the ongoing thought process of the poetic voice:

> Take all my loves, my love, yea, take them all
> (Sonnet 40, l. 1)

> If there be nothing new, but that which is
> (Sonnet 59, l. 1)

> Alas, 'tis true, I have gone here and there
> (Sonnet 110, l. 1)

> O call me not to justify the wrong
> (Sonnet 139, l. 1)

The juxtaposition of the first and last lines also has a powerful effect on the artistry of the collection as a progressive experience. For instance, Sonnet 18 which ends with a confident affirmation of its own life-giving empowerment seems immediately to be overtaken by the threat of Time, ravaging the lover like a lion:

> So long lives this, and this gives life to thee.
> (Sonnet 18, l. 14)

> Devouring Time, blunt thou the lion's paws.
> (Sonnet 19, l. 1)

The richness of the transitional space after each sonnet varies throughout the collection, but at times it is possible to imagine the lover replying to the poet and so prompting the sonnet which follows. The transition between Sonnets 104 and 105, for instance, is one of qualification, as if the lover might have raised an objection to the poet's closing hyperbole:

> Ere you were born was beauty's summer dead.
> (Sonnet 104, l. 14)

> Let not my love be called idolatry.
> (Sonnet 105, l. 1)

The impact of Shakespeare's use of rhyme in the Sonnets is largely determined by the juxtaposition of sound, sense, and metre. The first quatrain of Sonnet 8 perfectly exemplifies the intricate relationship between these three almost infinite variables:

> Music to hear, why hear'st thou music sadly?
> Sweets with sweets war not, joy delights in joy:
> Why lov'st thou that which thou receiv'st not gladly,
> Or else receiv'st with pleasure thine annoy?
>
> (Sonnet 8, ll. 1–4)

The bitter-sweet proposition of the opening line and the adverb 'sadly' make the line longer by one syllable, prolonging a pervasive feeling of melancholy. The metre places stress on the repeated 'music' and the verb 'to hear'. It is as if the lover's initial response to the music might have been different before the effect arrived at by the end of the line. The impact of the dramatic present tense, which gives an immediacy to nearly all the sonnets (Nos. 17 and 98 are good examples of the future and past tenses, respectively), suspends the question raised in the first line to take the reader/lover through the contrast of 'sweets' and 'joy' in line 2. Again there is repetition and balance in 'sweets' and 'joy', softening the impact of 'war not' and suggesting that repetition might erase the melancholy currently observed. The mainly monosyllabic second line is ignited by the disyllabic 'delights' which leads on to further 'joy', sharply set against 'sadly' which rules over the top of it, and prompts the second question in lines 3 and 4. Line 3 varies the expectation of balance through repetition with the construction 'lov'st thou that which thou receiv'st'. The first rhyme occurs with 'not gladly', a heartbreaking development and transference which takes the reader back to 'sadly' in line 1 as the melancholic music continues. Line 4 takes the question further and mildly accuses the lover of contrariness, of receiving annoyance 'with pleasure'. At the same time as the object of the second line becomes clear, 'thine annoy', so chimes the second rhyme, taking the reader back to 'joy', now left a little further behind, but retrospectively received 'with pleasure' because of the rhyming sound and contrasting lengths of lines 1 and 3, lines 2 and 4.

> If the true concord of well-tunèd sounds
> By unions married do offend thine ear,
> They do but sweetly chide thee, who confounds

> In singleness the parts that thou shouldst bear.
> Mark how one string, sweet husband to another,
> Strikes each in each by mutual ordering;
> Resembling sire, and child, and happy mother,
> Who all in one, one pleasing note do sing:
>> Whose speechless song being many, seeming one,
>> Sings this to thee, 'Thou single wilt prove none.'
>
> (Sonnet 8, ll. 5–14)

The rest of the poem's rhymes map other satisfying relationships of sound and sense across its metrically taut and varied structural beat: 'sounds'/'confounds', 'ear'/'bear', 'another'/'mother' (both adding extra syllables to lines about procreation and extending the family), 'ordering'/'sing' and finally rhyming 'one' with 'none'. Part of the cumulative impact is the awareness that the progressive sound and sense of the sonnet is as interconnected as the musical notes it describes, singing and ordering, procreating more notes out of itself, all mathematically arranged to an irrevocable, harmonious effect. The numerological perspective of Shakespeare's sonnets, which can often seem to be an imperative which is proved by degrees of coincidences, here seems utterly appropriate as Sonnet 8, the number of musical notes in a complete octave, makes the sweet and bitter concords and discords of desire attune to the procreation of children. (Other numerological interpretations are discussed in Chapter 4.)

The musical sounds of Sonnet 8 are prescribed by its sense, rhyme, and metre. Another variable which determines a sonnet's aural impact is punctuation, but this can sometimes rely more on interpretation than on prescription. John Barton, the Shakespeare director and co-founder of the Royal Shakespeare Company, has used the Sonnets extensively when working with actors' voices and their approach to Shakespearian verse. One of his favourite exercises is to strip a sonnet of its punctuation and then to explore the many different ways that it might sound and mean. The actor-reader must determine the length of pauses and sense for themselves as a series of different pathways and emphases are explored and articulated. Like Sonnet 8, the rest of the sonnets make many memorable sounds throughout their duration. In 'For as you were when first your eye I eyed' (Sonnet 104, l. 2), 'eye I eyed' keeps the reader's mouth open to repeat the same sound but with a clear variety of progressive meaning. Sonnet 129 can seem exhausting as the words and sounds hunt themselves through one twelve-line-long sentence and a couplet:

> Past reason hunted, and no sooner had,
> Past reason hated as a swallowed bait.
>
> > (Sonnet 129, ll. 6–7).

Sonnet 81 makes explicit the acute awareness of the poetic voice to the power and articulation of sound. Reverberating across the ages in a variety of mouths, Sonnet 81's aural, oral, and visual demands make the lover alive in language and therefore in the literal breathing of all future readers:

> Your monument shall be my gentle verse,
> Which eyes not yet created shall o'er-read,
> And tongues-to-be your being shall rehearse,
> When all the breathers of this world are dead.
> > You still shall live (such virtue hath my pen)
> > Where breath most breathes, even in the mouths of men.
>
> > > (ll. 9–14)

The repetition of verbal power is present too in the hundreds, possibly thousands, of semantic echoes within Shakespeare's sonnets. A Shakespeare concordance can easily help to plot repeated words through the collection.

A concentrated illustration of how ideas echo and develop is provided by Sonnets 55 to 60 which focus intently on the varying effects of mutability. Sonnet 55 monumentalizes the lover as an eternal statue, Sonnets 56–8 grant the lover a new lease of freedom, placing him or her in charge of time. In Sonnet 56, the most the poet expects of his lover is to look ahead to tomorrow. The next day will always bring the possibility that their love will be re-created. In Sonnet 57, the lover commands the present moment with absolute mastery. The poet becomes like a slave that will stay his lover's pleasure. Sonnet 58 is concerned with the perpetual hell of waiting, as the poet makes another determined attempt to control time himself. The positioning of Sonnet 59 creates a moment in which time seems to stop. From the reflections on eternity in Sonnet 55, to the poet giving the control of time to his lover (Sonnets 56 and 57) and only being able to wait

(Sonnet 58), Shakespeare now classes himself among 'the wits of former days' (Sonnet 59, l. 13). Sonnet 59 attempts to make the past real again and Shakespeare, as John Kerrigan remarks, seeks to 'redeem time by recouping the past in the present' (Kerrigan, p. 45). Time, of course, cannot be redeemed, not even through the use of verbal and intellectual echoes. Instead, these sonnets realize that there is only the calm and gradual erosion of the present as any attempts to assuage the inevitability of Time in Sonnets 55–9 break with the waves of Sonnet 60:

> Like as the waves make towards the pebbled shore,
> So do our minutes hasten to their end;
> Each changing place with that which goes before,
> In sequent toil all forwards do contend.
>
> (Sonnet 60, ll. 1–4)

So, to return to the beginning of this chapter and Sonnet 76, Shakespeare is 'dressing old words' and ideas anew as they transmutate like the sounds of waves and undergo sea changes and gradual erosion which impact on the lover's and the reader's minds. The artistry of these poems must in the end be felt and experienced both in the general and the particular. Their substance, like that of the lover and the implied reader—that imagined and transcendent image we might measure against ourselves as we read through the collection—continues to cast before us what Sonnet 53 calls 'millions of strange shadows'.

Concerns of the Sonnets

The Sonnets repeat strands of emotions and ideas, emphasizing a polyphony of attitudes and approaches to love rather than working through any single one. However, it is part of the Sonnets' fascination that they invite readers to identify connecting interpretative threads. In his modestly entitled *An Essay on Shakespeare's Sonnets*, Stephen Booth voices the critical, and indeed human, desire to unify experience:

Perhaps the happiest moment the human mind ever knows is the moment when it senses the presence of order and coherence—and before it realizes the particular nature (and so the particular limits) of the perception. . . . As he reads through the 1609 sequence, a reader's mind is constantly poised on just such a threshold to comprehension. The source of that pleasurable sense of increased mental range is the same multitude of frames of reference that frustrate him when he looks for a single label or formula by which his mind may take personal possession of the sonnets. (Booth, *Essay*, p. 14)

Although multivocal in their scope, the Sonnets amplify a number of dominant themes and concerns which are revisited and reinvented throughout all 154 of them. Ultimately it is impossible to divorce what poems are about from the way in which they are written. Nevertheless, in this chapter we wish, however artificially, to isolate some of the principal concerns of the Sonnets if only as a way of drawing attention to the diversity and complexity of the variations that they play on the theme of love.

Time, Image, and Verse

The passage of Time, the attempt to regain the past, to control the present, and to combat Time's destructive effects, preoccupies the poet in many of the sonnets. Closely related to the poet's desire at once to enjoy the passing flux of the present moment and for time to stand still is the will for immortality both of the verse and of the beloved:

> His beauty shall in these black lines be seen,
> And they shall live, and he in them still green.
>
> (Sonnet 63, 13–14)

The poet's self-conscious reference to the actual physical appearance of his 'black lines' is here related to, and contrasted with, the power of language to push its associative and semantic value beyond the immediate and physically bound realm of manuscript and print to the imaginative resonance of words themselves. At the end of this poem the progression of black lines which make up the sonnet for the reader are turned green and independently spring-like. The end of Sonnet 18 also reminds the reader of the life-giving power of poetry:

> So long as men can breathe or eyes can see,
> So long lives this, and this gives life to thee.
>
> (Sonnet 18, ll. 13–14)

or, as in Sonnet 19:

> Yet do thy worst, old Time: despite thy wrong,
> My love shall in my verse ever live young.
>
> (Sonnet 19, ll. 13–14)

(Sonnets 15, 100, and 107 provide further comparisons and examples.)

Time's abyss yawns in the face of any attempt to conquer it. The inherent contradiction in the poet's efforts is that by making the reader more aware of Time in his aspiration to overcome it, he also draws attention to the mutability of all creation. It is rather like the satirical anecdote that the melancholy fool Jaques relates in *As You Like It* in which just looking at a watch can encourage a meditation on mortality:

> 'Tis but an hour ago since it was nine,
> And after one hour more 'twill be eleven.
> And so from hour to hour we ripe and ripe,
> And then from hour to hour we rot and rot.

> (2.6.24–7)

Only by emphasizing his inevitable failure, however, can the poet successfully articulate his love which 'among the wastes of time must go' (Sonnet 12, l. 10).

Sonnets 1–17 are concerned with procreation, with breeding and re-creating the image of oneself in another living and autonomous being in order to combat the ravages of Time and so vicariously to achieve everlasting life. In this respect they are grounded firmly in the Platonic ideal of procreative love expressed in the *Symposium*, 'because procreation is the nearest thing to perpetuity and immortality that a mortal being can attain'.[1] It is through procreation that Shakespeare wills the re-creation and transcendence of his lover through time.

A prime example of this is the transition of thought between Sonnets 2 and 3. In the sestet of Sonnet 2 Shakespeare imagines the beloved reflecting on the joys of parenthood, as intimations of immortality:

> How much more praise deserved thy beauty's use,
> If thou couldst answer 'This fair child of mine
> Shall sum my count, and make my old excuse,'
> Proving his beauty by succession thine.
>   This were to be new made when thou art old,
>   And see thy blood warm when thou feel'st it cold.

> (ll. 9–14)

The emphasis here is on new life, making the old young again and rekindling the cold. In Sonnet 3, this seemingly straightforward idea develops more fully and becomes much more complicated. This sonnet begins with a command which controls not only the lover, but the reader of the sonnet as well:

> Look in thy glass and tell the face thou viewest
> Now is the time that face should form another.

> (ll. 1–2)

Not only this, but the image of the lover has now been split, multiplied by the mirror, reflected, and re-created. This sonnet also introduces the beloved's mother who 'Calls back the lovely April of her prime' (l. 10) through her child's image. Procreation thus provides the possibility of new vision in terms of how one's image is perceived and the relationships which surround it. By Sonnet 3, these have become multi-focused, the lover's reflection also leading on to Sonnets 4, 5, 6, and 7 which all declare that mortal beauty should increase rather than being narcissistically self-absorbed. The mirror serves at once as a reminder to procreate and as a warning against the single, lonely life. It is in Sonnet 11 that Shakespeare first relates the process of procreation to his own poetic craft. Shakespeare encourages his lover that Nature

> . . . carved thee for her seal, and meant thereby,
> Thou shouldst print more, not let that copy die.
>
> (ll. 13–14)

By self-referral to the physicality of his own text, Shakespeare begins to turn from procreative concerns to his own creativity; from the world to the word.

In Sonnets 12 and 14, Shakespeare considers the outward, physical world and the effect that it has upon his lover: 'the brave day sunk in hideous night' (Sonnet 12, l. 2), 'Of plagues, of dearths, or season's quality' (Sonnet 14, l. 4) and seems to realize that procreation is not sufficient in itself to ensure the re-creation of his lover: poetry must be able to do more. The first seventeen sonnets lead towards the realization that there is 'breed' to brave Time (Sonnet 12, ll. 13–14) and affirm the power of language as an additional challenge. By Sonnet 17, the possibility of a child is equated with the power of rhyme itself:

> But were some child of yours alive that time,
> You should live twice, in it, and in my rhyme.
>
> (ll. 13–14)

The challenge has now become twofold: to make the lover present in the verse itself, as well as in some future child. Shakespeare has succeeded in uniting the two dimensions of love that Plato perceived as being separate: 'there are some whose creative desire is of the soul, and who long to beget spiritually, not physically, the progeny which it is the nature of the soul to create and bring to birth'.[2] Shakespeare is able to envisage both the procreative and the spiritual as coexistent in his beloved. By the end of the procreation sonnets, he succeeds in re-creating the image of the lover as a dramatic presence in the verse, and at the end of Sonnet 17, it is as if the lover becomes present in the sound of the rhyming couplet itself.

Time can also be felt through the changing seasons, reference to which is another way in which the poet attempts to evoke the image and presence of the lover. In Sonnet 98 (and in a similar way in Sonnet 113), the poet plays with his absent lover's imagined shadow in the natural world made beautiful by the spring and by the seemingly incidental directness of the poetic diction:

> From you have I been absent in the spring
> When proud-pied April (dressed in all his trim)
> Hath put a spirit of youth in every thing
>
> (Sonnet 98, ll. 1–3).

The transcendent power of youth is also the argument of Sonnet 104 which suggests a three-year time frame during which the intensity of the love described has been felt.

> Three winters cold
> Have from the forests shook three summers' pride,
> Three beauteous springs to yellow autumn turned
> In process of the seasons have I seen,
> Three April perfumes in three hot Junes burned,
> Since first I saw you fresh, which yet are green.
>
> (Sonnet 104, ll. 3–8)

The lover has not aged and the relationship still seems as young and as new as when it first began: 'Ere you were born was beauty's summer dead' (l. 14). From procreation, through the many attempts to combat time, the poetic voice, becoming Canute-like, shows the pointlessness of its own endeavour. By the time we reach Sonnet 126, with its empty brackets, it is as if the poet has found a different poetic form to warn the lover and the reader of the effects of Time to which even the loveliest of creations must eventually be rendered and made account of in death, and in the face of which words and language are annihilated.

Desire

The first line of Shakespeare's Sonnet 1, 'From fairest creatures we desire increase', opens the collection with the inclusive assumption that 'we' (the reader, the addressee and the poet, or everyone) do desire to create more of the superlative beauty we see around us. Just as the lover seems to encompass the classical archetypes of the objects of both male and female desire in the images of Helen and Adonis (Sonnet 53), so too does the whole collection seem to present seemingly infinite possibilities of desire both spiritual and physical. It is anachronistic to use the terms heterosexual, homosexual, and bisexual since they did not exist in the seventeenth century and can often obstruct access to an understanding of early modern sexualities. Sexual relationships between persons of the same sex could be outlawed as 'sodomy' (a term used to cover a multitude of different sins) and punishable by death. The critical inquiries of Bruce R. Smith show that no 'rigid distinction between male friendship and male homosexuality' was made in Shakespeare's time and has only emerged in Western culture within the last two hundred years.[3] The poetic voice in the Sonnets speaks for any kind of sexuality in physical and spiritual manifestations without locating any fixed definitions. There is too an exploration of friendship which runs parallel to the sexual desire of these poems and sometimes becomes fused with it. As Paul Hammond comments: 'in the early modern period these words "friend" and "lover" each had a wide semantic field, and the two fields overlapped' (*Figuring Sex*, p. 18). 'Friend' could be used as a socially polite form of address to strangers and inferiors as well as carrying the same sense of social and emotional intimacy that it has today; it could also mean lover. Michel de Montaigne's essay 'On Friendship' (or 'On Affectionate Relationships'), describes friendship as a deeply spiritual and emotional but explicitly non-sexual attachment:

As for the rest, those we ordinarily call friends and amities are but acquaintances and familiarities, tied together by some occasions, or commodities, by means whereof our minds are entertained.

In the amity I speak of, they intermix and confound themselves one in the other with so universal a commixture that they wear out and can no more find the seam that hath conjoined them together. If a man urge me to tell wherefore I loved him, I feel it cannot be expressed, but by answering 'Because it was he, because it was my self.' ('Pourquoi je l'aimais ? Parce que c'était lui, parce que c'était moi.')[4]

The closeness of the relationship that Shakespeare expresses and explores in the Sonnets (Nos. 29 and 30, for example) can be compared to Montaigne's definitions. But it does not have to be. Similarly, 'lover' could mean a well-wisher, a person who loves and is loved, whilst implying a more sexual relationship as well. The word 'friend' and its cognates occurs nineteen times in the Sonnets: Nos. 29, 30 (twice), 31, 32, 42 (three times), 50, 82, 104, 110, 111, 133 (three times), 134, 144, and 149. The word 'lover' occurs in five sonnets: Nos. 31, 32, 55, 63, and 126. Meanings of the words change depending on how the reader chooses to define them. As Hammond asserts, 'ambiguity may be necessary, and definition may be undesirable or even dangerous' (*Figuring Sex*, p. 20).

Sex in the Sonnets is most immediately present in the poetic use of sexually explicit or suggestive language (love actually groans in Nos. 131 and 133, a sound associated with both gratification and despondency) and especially in the vilification of lust (Nos. 129 and 142) and the body of the mistress (Nos. 137, 142, 147–52). In the expression of desire, however, the Sonnets are more semantically unstable. Colin Burrow warns that to 'fix their sexuality is to seek to lock them in, where most, perhaps, they seek to be free' (p. 124). To fix is partly to locate and identify; a lot of potential freedom hangs on Burrow's use of 'perhaps': the freedom of sexuality and the freedom to desire. In some sonnets the poet is transfixed by obsession with the beloved (Nos. 27, 43, and 61 are all about the image of the lover keeping the poet and his imagination awake at night); others confront the arguments that might happen between two lovers and which love in some way resolves (Nos. 35, 40, 94, 131, 140); other sonnets describe the effect that separation has on desire (Nos. 36, 39, 87); some re-create the lover's image as a dramatic presence through desire (Nos. 97, 98, 113, 130); in some the poet separates mental from emotional faculties in articulating desire (Nos. 14, 24, 33, 46, 47, 119, 133, 141); some describe the palpable physical and emotional impact that desire has on the poet (Nos. 75, 80, 118, 129, 147); there is even a sense of resigned celibacy remembering former desire (Nos. 31, 73, 81); other poems consider desire in the face of death (Nos. 66, 71)—indeed so tortured is the poet in Sonnet 147 that 'Desire is death' (l. 8)—a total absorption of mortality in a destructive but still loving relationship which draws on the sense of death as orgasm—or vice versa.

The ways in which individual sonnets convey desire vary through-out the collection. Even within the small groups of examples given above it is not appropriate to expect that 'desire' (rather like the words 'friend' and 'lover') will necessarily have the same range of senses in all of the thirteen sonnets in which it is mentioned. Saturated with desire these sonnets remain, though, and erotic phrases stream throughout the collection: 'the sun | Delights to peep, to gaze therein on thee' (No. 24, ll. 11–12), 'all-too-precious you' (No. 86, l. 2), 'most most loving breast' (No. 110, l. 14), 'Incapable of more, replete with you' (No. 113, l. 13), 'To kiss the tender inward of thy hand' (No. 128, l. 6), and 'desire to be invited | To any sensual feast with thee alone' (No. 141, ll. 7–8). Questions of context will also affect how a reader interprets the poet's expression of desire, and how its articulation relates to friends and lovers.

What now follows is a consideration of desire in a single sonnet from which principles of interpretation might be transferred to others in the collection.

> When in the chronicle of wasted time
> I see descriptions of the fairest wights,
> And beauty making beautiful old rhyme
> In praise of ladies dead, and lovely knights;
> Then in the blazon of sweet beauty's best,
> Of hand, of foot, of lip, of eye, of brow,
> I see their antique pen would have expressed
> Even such a beauty as you master now.
> So all their praises are but prophecies
> Of this our time, all you prefiguring,
> And, for they looked but with divining eyes,
> They had not skill enough your worth to sing:
>   For we, which now behold these present days,
>   Have eyes to wonder, but lack tongues to praise.

(Sonnet 106)

The gender of Sonnet 106's addressee is indeterminate. It might be addressed to either a man or a woman by either an imaginary male or female poetic voice. The cumulative experience of the collection thus far has evoked much 'wasted time'; the preceding sonnets have to an extent chronicled this themselves, for example 'with old woes new wail my dear time's waste' (No. 30, l. 4). The poet describes reading descriptions of the most beautiful figures of the chivalric past, 'the fairest wights' (a self-consciously archaic word recalling Edmund Spenser's *Faerie Queene*). The phrase also recalls the 'fairest creatures' of Sonnet 1 from whom 'we desire increase' (l. 1). Other 'wights' in the Sonnets include Adonis and Helen in No. 53 (ll. 5, 7), ideals of male and female beauty from the classical past which when closely associated summon up a universality of desire, multi-focused in its sexual potential. Here the poet establishes a comparable context with 'ladies dead and lovely knights'. 'Lovely' could mean 'attracting love' as well as 'handsome' and here seems to favour and make desirable the knights over the 'ladies dead'. Although both might have their beauty recorded, 'in the blazon' perhaps more specifically indicates a coat of arms and so relates more to the masculine 'sweet beauty' of the knights. 'Of hand, of foot, of lip, of eye, of brow' takes the reader's eye over the imagined body of one of these ladies or knights (and is reminiscent of the fair Princess Catherine of France in *Henry V* who is taught the English words for hand, fingers, nails, arm, elbow, neck, chin, foot, and dress by her maid Alice in 3.4). In Gregory Woods's reading of this line,[5] Shakespeare is offering an erotic and seductive description of the body of his male lover to the reader. The reference to 'antique pen' presents another male dimension in its reference to the male poets who wrote about these same 'wights'; 'pen' could also be suggestive of 'penis' which these knights would have used to further their beauty through procreating 'Even such a beauty as you master now'. As a verb, 'master' is also reminiscent of the poet's 'master-mistress' (Sonnet 20, l. 2), but here seems exclusively male. The work of all classical and courtly literature, and the world it inhabits, serves only to prefigure, divine, and prophesy the existence of the poet's lover. In the couplet the poet describes the effect of the presentness of the lover. It is no longer a case of reading or speaking, but looking, staring, and being silent. The sonnet ends with the lover and the poet disappearing into what might be a supposed physical rather than purely literary consummation. Tongues can be used in different ways between lovers, after all.

Language of Sexuality

From desire it is but a short step to fulfilment. In Chapter 2 we noted that one of the features of Shakespeare's collection that most distinguishes it from others of the period is its frankness about sex. Several of the poems include unmistakable reference to sexual organs and activity; in others the sex is, if anything, all the more apparent by being lightly veiled under a thin cover of wordplay. And, as Paul Hammond puts it, 'The language of the *Sonnets* frequently has sexual connotations which are not consolidated into puns or metaphors' (*Figuring Sex*, p. 70).

In writing about the first seventeen sonnets in the earlier part of this chapter we have concentrated on their concern with procreation as a means of overcoming the effects of time and on the way in which the poet's art can assist in this endeavour. To an extent these are metaphysical poems, but sex is never far away. In Sonnet 1 there is a veiled allusion to masturbation as the poet deplores the young man's feeding his 'light's flame with self-substantial fuel' (l. 6), which may imply that he pleasures himself by producing his own semen and not using it for procreation. And later the poet accuses the young man that he 'Within thine own bud buriest thy content' (l. 11): semen is produced from the glans ('bud') of the young man's penis only for his own pleasure, and thus is 'buried' without progeny. In Sonnet 4, too, the young man is accused of 'having traffic with thyself alone' (l. 9). The laddish intimacy of these remarks is not easy to reconcile with the notion that the poet is writing to someone he scarcely knows on commission from a parent impatient to have grandchildren, as scholars taking a biographical approach have often suggested. In Sonnet 3 the phrase 'tillage of thy husbandry' (l. 6) anticipates the coarse realism of Agrippa's remark about Caesar's relations with Cleopatra: 'He ploughed her and she cropped' (*Antony and Cleopatra*, 2.2.235). The image of 'summer's distillation left | A liquid prisoner pent in walls of glass' in Sonnet 5 (ll. 9–10), where there is no overt sexual referent, shades into sexuality in the following poem's delicate but unmistakable identification of a potential bride's vagina as 'some vial', which the young man may 'Make sweet', and of his semen as 'beauty's treasure' with which he may 'treasure . . . some place . . . ere it be self-killed' (Sonnet 6, ll. 3–4)—i. e. has lost its potency.

> 20
>
> A Womans face with natures owne hand painted,
>   Haſte thou the Maſter Miſtris of my paſſion,
> A womans gentle hart but not acquainted
> With ſhifting change as is falſe womens faſhion,
> An eye more bright then theirs,leſſe falſe in rowling:
> Gilding the obiect where-vpon it gazeth,
> A man in hew all *Hews* in his controwling,
> Which ſteales mens eyes and womens ſoules amaſeth.
> And for a woman wert thou firſt created,
> Till nature as ſhe wrought thee fell a dotinge,
> And by addition me of thee defeated,
> By adding one thing to my purpoſe nothing.
>   But ſince ſhe prickt thee out for womens pleaſure,
>   Mine be thy loue and thy loues vſe their treaſure.

Fig. 8. The sexual resonances of Sonnet 20 have made it one of the most intensively discussed of the Sonnets. Do the italicization and capitalization of the word *Hews* give a clue to the identity of its recipient?

The sonnet most frequently discussed in relation to the poet's sexuality is Sonnet 20, and the complexities of its interpretation demand detailed consideration.

The first lines as printed in the Quarto read:

> A Womans face with natures owne hand painted,
> Haste thou the Master Mistris of my passion,

The first line may simply mean that the friend looks more like a woman who needs no adornment from cosmetics than like a man, but presumably also implies that this makes him more attractive to the poet than if he were more masculine in appearance. His androgyny is part of his appeal. Since the friend is male he is master of the poet's 'passion' (meaning 'love', with undertones of 'suffering' and even of his verses, since 'passion' could mean a passionate speech). He is also mistress of the poet's passion because he is loved as another man might love a woman. But the phrase may also mean, as Burrow points out, 'sovereign'—i. e. supreme—'mistress', with even more emphasis on his femininity. The next two lines extend the comparison with a woman's face to the friend's personality—'A womans gentle hart'—but misogynistically elevate him above the female stereotype because he is 'not acquainted | With shifting change as is false womens fashion'.

This is perhaps the most explicit expression of generalized misogyny in the sonnets. The theme continues in 'An eye more bright then theirs, lesse fals in rowling: | Gilding the obiect where-vpon it gazeth', where 'Gilding' retrospectively gives to 'bright' an active sense, implying that the brightness of the friend's eye confers a similar quality on the object of its gaze. Adoration continues with 'A man in hew all *Hews* in his controwling, | Which steales mens eyes and womens soules amaseth'.

'Hew' is not the most obvious word to refer to the friend's appearance, and its italicization and capitalization on its second appearance have understandably raised the suspicion that it is used punningly, as certainly is *Will* elsewhere. If this is so the word must have held private significance for the poet and, presumably, his addressee. Malone's suggestion, developed by Oscar Wilde, that 'Hughes' is this friend's surname is perhaps not entirely wide of the mark. But other words where a pun seems less likely are similarly treated in the Quarto: '*Rose*' (No. 1, l. 2), '*Audit*' (No. 4, l. 12), the proper names *Adonis* and *Hellens*, along with *Grecian* (No. 53, ll. 5, 7, and 8), *Statues* and *Mars* (No. 55, ll. 5 and 7), *Intrim* (No. 56, l. 9), *Alien* (No. 78, l. 3), *Eaues* (No. 93, l. 13), *Saturne* (No. 98, l. 4), *Satire* (No. 100, l. 11), *Philomell* (No. 102, l. 7), *Autumne* (No. 104, l. 5), *Abisme* (No. 112, l. 9), *Alcumie* (No. 114, l. 4), *Syren* (No. 119, l. 1), *Heriticke* (No. 124, l. 9), *Informer* (No. 125, l. 13), *Audite* and *Quietus* (No. 126, ll. 11 and 12), '*will*' variously in Nos. 135, 136, and 143, and *Cupid, Dyans,* and *Cupid* (Nos. 153, ll. 1, 2, 14). Most of these instances are consonant with normal printer's practice for proper names and for words of foreign origin (like *Statues* and *Quietus*) felt not to be fully anglicized, but '*Rose*' in Sonnet 1 has also been interpreted as a pun on Southampton's family name 'Wriothesley', which could be pronounced 'Rose-ly'. Just about enough of the other words are commonplace enough for us not to be sure that the italicization of 'hews'—a well-established word—is meaningful.

So far Sonnet 20 could be a love poem addressed to a man in which adoration of a male combined with denigration of females implies a same-sex passion, but this seems to be denied in the next lines:

> And for [i.e. as] a woman wert thou first created,
> Till nature as she wrought thee fell adotinge,

> And by addition me of thee defeated,
> By adding one thing to my purpose nothing.

(ll. 9–12)

Nature—who had (not) painted the youth's face, has cheated the poet of full possession of him by foolishly ('adotinge') adding to the created female body a 'thing'—slang for penis—which the poet can put to no purpose. The couplet uses a bawdy pun to reinforce the idea:

> But since she prickt thee out for womens pleasure,
> Mine be thy loue and thy loues vse their treasure.

(ll. 13–14)

One sense of 'prick out' is 'select', but 'prick' as penis is punned upon in several Shakespeare plays, and there is no avoiding its double meaning here. So the poem ends by imploring the young man still to endow the poet with his love even though the existence of the beloved's penis, designed to give sexual pleasure to women, means that the physical expression ('use') of that love can only enrich women.

Or does it? At least since the 1960s reasons have been brought forward to argue that this sonnet does not necessarily deny the possibility of a sexual relationship. Paul Hammond remarks that 'the apparent denial of sexual interest in the youth is undone by a realization that "nothing" is slang for the female genitals' (*Figuring Sex,* p. 16), which would imply that the 'thing' added can please the poet in the way that a vagina would a woman. In a variation on this theme, Stephen Orgel argues that 'the "women's pleasure" the friend is "pricked out for" (i.e. selected for...) is not the pleasure he gives women but his ability to take pleasure as women do; "loves" in the last line is then not a possessive but a plural, and "use" is a verb—the line without its modern apostrophe need not be a renunciation at all: "let my love be yours, and let your loves make use of their treasure"'.[6] We find this interpretation difficult to accept, as it seems to require that 'pricked' means simply 'selected for' with no sexual pun. The sonnet's expression of sexual desire for the man, even if it cannot be consummated, is undeniable. The lover's prick is of use to women since it produces children—their 'treasure'—but is no less enjoyable for the poet. Whatever the poet says about this young man's prick, the earlier

Fig. 9. The poet addresses Sonnet 20 to 'the Master Mistris' of his 'passion', suggesting androgyny. This portrait, believed for centuries to depict a woman, Lady Norton, was only in 2002 identified as a portrait of the young Henry Wriothesley, third Earl of Southampton, to whom Shakespeare dedicated *Venus and Adonis* in 1593, and *The Rape of Lucrece* in 1594.

part of the poem shows that he finds the rest of him as attractive as he might expect himself to find a woman whom he might desire.

Notwithstanding the bawdiness of its phrasing, the expression of homoerotic desire in Sonnet 20 is romantic in its idealization of a youth's beauty of person and of character.

Sonnet 151, addressed to a woman, is more crudely physical in its expression of desire. The woman is a 'gentle cheater' (l. 3)—she has betrayed the poet with another man. So she has no right to blame the poet for any faults that he may show: 'urge not *my* amiss' (l. 3, our italics). Awareness of her sin absolves him of blame for his lust. Using metaphysical terminology akin to that of the religious sonnet, No. 146, he claims that his soul—the 'nobler part' of him in which his conscience resides—tells his body that it may justly 'Triumph in love' (ll. 7–8)—where 'love' seems almost indistinguishable from lust—in copulating with the woman. The language in which he writes of this is as far as it is possible to get from the conventions of sonnet literature. His 'flesh'—we may remember that Dogberry, in *Much Ado About Nothing*, claims to be 'as pretty a piece of flesh as any is in Messina' (4.2.79–80)— rises at the woman's name and points at her. The poet is proud of this 'pride' (l. 10)—his erect penis—and happy that it should be the woman's slave in becoming erect and detumescent in accordance with the waxing and waning of her desire. The couplet might almost be spoken by the penis itself: 'No want of conscience hold it that I call | Her "love", for whom I rise and fall' (ll. 13–14). The bawdy of this poem has been complicated—implausibly in our view—by recent interpreters' suggestions that the words 'conscience' (ll. 1, 2, and 13) and 'contented' (l. 11) may carry a sense of 'cunt' (e.g. Vendler, p. 129).

The poem we have just been discussing is characteristic of the sonnets in the second part of the collection in that as a group these are the frankest in their sexuality. In Sonnet 144—'Two loves I have, of comfort and despair'—one of the finest and at the same time most searingly bitter poems in the collection—the sexuality is both misogynistic and self-lacerating. It is a climactic poem in the sense that in it the poet directly confronts his conflicting desires for a male and a female. It does so in the form of a miniature morality play, rather like that played out in Lancelot's mind between his conscience and the devil in *The Merchant of Venice* (2.2.1–29). In keeping with this the imagery is in part religious. Here the male plays the role allotted to the soul in Sonnet 151, the female, the body. '[A] man right fair' is the poet's 'better angel' who brings him comfort; his 'worser' spirit who causes his despair is 'a woman coloured ill', a 'female evil' who, like the devil in a morality play, seeks to corrupt his 'saint to be a devil, | Wooing his purity with her foul pride' (ll. 3–8)—in this context 'pride' takes on the sense of sexual desire. The poet fears that his angelic friend has been lured into the woman's 'hell'—her vagina, but also recalling the exit on the medieval stage that symbolized the underworld. He will never be certain of this, the couplet says, 'Till my bad angel fire my good one out' (l. 14)—that is, till the woman rejects the man, blasting his penis out of her infected hell, and also till the man shows the burning symptoms of disease. The poem's formal perfection may suggest that the poet's feelings are fully under control, but their bitter intensity is apparent in the wordplay on both 'angel' and 'hell' in the sense of sexual organ, and in the implication of venereal disease in the word 'fire'.

Black Beauty

For all the occasional ferocity of their sexuality, not all the sonnets concerned with a woman are crudely denigratory in the manner of Sonnet 151. Although she is often characterized by the poet and has been regarded by later readers as primarily 'dark', metaphorically as well as actually, some of the poems speak deeply of love, and not simply of sexual love. Indeed some of them imply chaste, rejected love. The very first sonnet to be written, No. 127, has a 'once upon a time' quality in its opening: 'In the old age black was not counted fair'. It goes on to praise a woman for not following the fashion of attempting to disguise blackness by using cosmetics; in fact her black eyes and eyebrows seem to mourn for other women who, 'not born fair', give nature a bad reputation by creating a false beauty for themselves. The mourning blackness of his mistress's dark beauty becomes her so well that it persuades all who see her that this is what true beauty should be. This is a love poem, but the terms of contorted paradox in which it is expressed are a world away from the lyricism of many of the poems addressed to a young man.

The theme of mourning eyes is reprised in Sonnet 132, exceptionally in this collection a Petrarchan poem of a disdained lover, where the mistress's eyes show pity for the rejected lover's pain. Lyricism blossoms in long vowels, run-on lines, easy rhythms, and natural imagery as the poet rhapsodizes over the beauty of the woman's black eyes:

> And truly not the morning sun of heaven
> Better becomes the grey cheeks of the east,
> Nor that full star that ushers in the even
> Doth half that glory to the sober west
> As those two mourning eyes become thy face.
>
> (ll. 5–9)

Now he is willing to swear that 'beauty herself is black, | And all they foul that thy complexion lack' (ll. 13–14). Less anguished praise of the mistress comes in Sonnet 128, in which the poet watches her playing a keyboard instrument (though nothing specifically identifies the addressee as a female).

In less complimentary style, the elegantly shaped Sonnet 138 ('When my love swears that she is made of truth, | I do believe her though I know she lies . . .') implies a sexual relationship that is far from ideal in mutuality. The poet and his mistress devise a strategy of putting up with each other's weaknesses by ignoring the truth: 'Therefore I lie with her, and she with me, | And in our faults by lies we flattered be' (ll. 13–14). And still more bitterly, other poems see a mistress's blackness as a true reflection of her character, playing with notions of the difference between inner and outward qualities defined by Viola in *Twelfth Night*:

> There is a fair behaviour in thee, captain,
> And though that nature with a beauteous wall
> Doth oft close in pollution, yet of thee
> I will believe thou hast a mind that suits
> With this thy fair and outward character.
>
> (1.2.43–7)

So Sonnet 131, in which the poet declares that his 'dear doting heart' sees a woman as 'the fairest and most precious jewel' (ll. 3–4) even though she is far from universally admired for beauty, concludes that the slander that she cannot make men fall in love with her results from the blackness of her deeds: 'In nothing art thou black save in thy deeds' (l. 13). It is a strange love poem in which a lover feels himself in a minority in admiring his mistress's face, and goes on to declare that in any case his eccentric admiration of her exterior is belied by her deplorable inner qualities.

The poet's pain is at its most intense in the poems (Sonnets 133–6 and 144) in which he writes of a love triangle involving himself, his mistress, and a young man, his 'sweet'st friend' (as we have seen, 'friend' could have a wide range of connotations) and 'next self' (Sonnet 133, ll. 4, 6). In Sonnet 133 ('Beshrew that heart...'), which seems to run on from Sonnet 132, the woman is tyrannizing over both of them. We are presumably intended to understand that she is rejecting both their advances, that the young man has broken with the poet ('Of him, myself, and thee I am forsaken', l. 7) and that the poet is nobly offering to sacrifice himself for his friend—'my friend's heart let my poor heart bail' (l. 10) seems to mean 'let my heart stand bail for my friend's and go to prison in place of him'—that is, he will give up his claims to the woman if she satisfies his friend. At first he thinks that this means the woman cannot 'use rigour' (l. 12)—be harsh—since the friend's heart will be guarded by his own; but then, contortedly, he argues that after all she will still be in charge, because his own heart (which guards his friend's) is itself in subjection to her.

In the next poem she has imprisoned both the friend and the poet, who is regretting his magnanimity: 'Him have I lost, thou hast both him and me; | He pays the whole, and yet I am not free' (Sonnet 134, ll. 13–14). Now he is in total subjection to her. This sonnet leads into the 'Will' poems (Sonnets 135 and 136), with their multiple obsessive puns, discussed in Chapter 4, above, in which the poet is regretting that the woman who now has her 'Will' will not 'have' him too. Her possession of the beloved is evident too in Sonnet 139, but the poet can still address her as 'Dear heart' and clearly still spends time with her.

In spite of recurring themes of servitude, self-abasement, self-loathing for sexual obsession for a woman he knows to be unfaithful, self-blame for his own faults—the addressee's lips have 'sealed false bonds of love *as oft as mine*' (Sonnet 142, l. 7, our italics)—the attitudes to love in these poems are so diverse and self-contradictory that it would be wrong to yield to the temptation to try to form from them a pattern in which true love, at first unrequited, passes through slow disillusionment, acknowledgement of folly, discovery of infidelity, sexual nausea, to total rejection. The poems constitute not a story of love corroded and denied, but a series of episodes, like snapshots taken at different times, some independent, some linked, that bear witness more to the suffering that love can inflict than to the joys it can confer.

The Sonnets as Theatre

Shakespeare's sonnets are as close as we can get to being the private poems of an otherwise public writer. His verse narratives, *Venus and Adonis* (1593) and *The Rape of Lucrece* (1594), were, everything suggests, set into type at his desire soon after he wrote them. His enigmatic, haunting, and esoteric short poem 'The Phoenix and Turtle' (or 'Let the Bird of Loudest Lay') was published in 1601 as part of an appendix to a volume of poems called *Love's Martyr* by the obscure Robert Chester, no doubt with Shakespeare's approval. And though only half of his plays appeared in print while he was alive, all of them were published by performance, the medium that he appears to have preferred for them.

By contrast, we know that sonnets written by him circulated among his 'private' friends long before any appeared in print, and there is no certainty that he was responsible for the eventual publication of the collection in 1609. Yet he seems to have gone on tinkering with them, adding to them, and ordering them over a period of many years. Clearly they meant a lot to him. During the whole of this time he was active as a writer for the theatre, and it is not surprising that both the poetic form of the sonnet, their thematic concerns, and the materials out of which his sonnets are composed form part of the woof and warp of his plays. The work of G. K. Hunter, M. M. Mahood, Roger Warren, and David Schalkwyk, mentioned in the Further Reading section, below, provides absorbing and useful studies of this topic. In this chapter we want to discuss aspects of the relationship between Shakespeare the private poet and Shakespeare the writer for the theatre. In doing so we will consider the way ideas about the theatre impact on Shakespeare's depiction of love and the use of the sonnet form within Shakespeare's plays, as well as the creative and thematic relationships that Shakespeare explores between his sonnets and his drama.

Theatre in the Sonnets

The Sonnets make use of theatrical metaphor in order to explore the re-creation of the lover's image which is constantly being re-dressed and re-presented in terms of perception, spectacle, performance, disguise, and self-conscious, as well as dramatic, utterance. The impression conveyed, far from being one of cohesive, biographical selves, is one in which identity and image are created, interrogated, and re-created by the gamut of experiences encountered. A deconstructionist critic, Ralph Flores, believes the Sonnets create space for Shakespeare to probe 'the conditions of theatre in ways which would be difficult, if not impossible, on the physical stage'.[1] Theatrical display of the lover's image runs throughout the collection and provides ways for Shakespeare to revitalize and vary his poetic technique. The beloved, like the dramatic art itself, is made inextricable from the present moment and is vulnerable to real and perceived change.

In Sonnet 15, for example, the universe is compared to a theatre:

> When I consider everything that grows
> Holds in perfection but a little moment,
> That this huge stage presenteth naught but shows
> Whereon the stars in secret influence comment;....
>
> (ll.1–4)

Here, the stars are audience to the performance of the poet and his lover, whose roles, though brief, are impressive enough to be comprehended by the unknowable, 'secret' night. Human existence on Shakespeare's stage world flickers between entrance and exit—the perfection of 'but a little moment'—and provides reason enough to strive for the exalted optimism which prevails throughout this sonnet, the final couplet promising that such moments will be forever newly engrafted and evolve upon 'this huge stage'. The use of the theatrical metaphor in Sonnet 15 serves to impress upon the reader the idea of the lover's image being re-created in the present moment while the sonnet itself is being read.

Sonnet 23 claims a different dramatic focus. Like a dull actor now, like Coriolanus, Shakespeare claims to have forgotten his part and is out 'Even to a full disgrace' (*Coriolanus*, 5.3.40–2). Or, is he like one that overacts?

> As an unperfect actor on the stage,
> Who with his fear is put besides his part,
> Or some fierce thing replete with too much rage
> Whose strength's abundance weakens his own heart;....
>
> (Sonnet 23, ll. 1–4)

Either way, Shakespeare draws comparison from the theatre to convey the sense of his impotence in performing the 'perfect ceremony of love's right' (l. 6). Instead, the lover/reader must read beyond such performative utterance, between the lines of the sonnet, in the silences between the words, to understand the poet's love. Like Cordelia, Shakespeare points us to the 'nothing' of his 'silent love' (that is his inability to express love's inexpressibility) instead of to some great speech. Sonnet 23 questions both the limits of theatre and the limits of language. Here, the creation of the lover's image and its presence lies beyond that which is presented on the page and in what our post-Stanislavskian world calls the subtext:

> O, learn to read what silent love hath writ;
> To hear with eyes belongs to love's fine wit.
>
> (ll. 13–14)

Even at its most heightened, Sonnet 23 seems to recognize that language itself, like a performed image, is only ever a metaphor of a Platonic 'reality' beyond, which finds fullest expression in the presence of, and when the poet is reacting to, the beloved.

Other examples which show the variety of theatrical metaphors to be found in the Sonnets might include Nos. 53, 113, 128, and 144. Here, the image of the lover is in flux, constantly changing within a complex refraction of perspectives and possibilities that fall naturally upon him/her:

> What is your substance, whereof are you made,
> That millions of strange shadows on you tend?
> Since everyone hath, everyone, one shade,
> And you, but one, can every shadow lend
>
> (Sonnet 53, ll. 1–4)

Shadows and shades were interchangeable terms for actors and the effects of acting for Shakespeare. As in Sonnet 98, Shakespeare is playing with the varying effects of shadow, entranced by the shades of light which commune with and re-create his lover's image, as he/she plays at being Adonis and Helen (Sonnet 53, ll. 5 and 7). If read biographically, this sonnet might even refer to a boy actor whom Shakespeare had seen playing both young men and women. In Sonnet 113, the lover becomes omnipresent in what seems like a performance of Nature. The poet's sensory experience reinvents images of the lover in every changing scene:

> For if it see the rud'st or gentlest sight,
> The most sweet-favour or deformed'st creature,
> The mountain, or the sea, the day, or night,
> The crow, or dove, it shapes them to your feature.
>
> (ll. 9–12)

By this stage in the collection the reader has already encountered the sonnets which might refer to the craft of the dramatist as the poet-lover confesses to having made himself 'a motley to the view' (No. 110, l. 2). He is like a theatrical fool, at once signifying everything and nothing, whose identity 'like the dyer's hand' (No. 111, l. 7) is constantly recast in various shades, colours and masks, depending on the moment.

In Sonnet 128, the poet watches his lover play music on a keyboard and becomes caught up in a live moment of performance. The instrument is caressed by the beloved's fingers, an experience loaded with sexual desire and allusion:

> To be so tickled, they would change their state
> And situation with those dancing chips
> O'er whom thy fingers walk with gentle gait,
> Making dead wood more blest than living lips.

> Since saucy jacks so happy are in this,
> Give them thy fingers, me thy lips to kiss.
>
> (Sonnet 128, ll. 9–14)

Sonnet 128 not only appreciates a performance given by the lover (who could be male or female) but admits the poet's desire to be at the very heart of that same creative experience. The sensual touch of his lover's fingers seems to make the poetic voice laugh at the end of this sonnet as Shakespeare refers to the tickling of the instrument's keys, the 'saucy jacks' which like sexual organs can move and respond to the power of a lover's nimble and caressing hands. The poet is utterly engrossed in the lover's movement, creativity, and presence as a performer. The musical, rather than the explicitly theatrical, allusion again implores the reader to 'hear with eyes' and so refers us back to Sonnet 23.

The poet becomes an Everyman figure in Sonnet 144 and imagines his two lovers as good and bad angels. The dramatic scenario presents 'a man right fair' (l. 3) being tempted away 'to hell, my female evil' (l. 5). Sonnet 144, though, unlike its medieval forebears, leaves this trial frustratingly unresolved. Rather, it calls to mind the many individual depictions of emotional drama which have taken place in the Sonnets thus far. Here Shakespeare presents the lover/reader with an ongoing dramatic narrative, empowering us to imagine the poetic voice perpetually frustrated and out of control:

> Yet this shall I ne'er know, but live in doubt
> Till my bad angel fire my good one out.
>
> (Sonnet 144, ll. 13–14)

Through theatrical metaphor, the Sonnets engage the reader in moments of re-creation which develop or transform the lover's image. Such moments reinvigorate the collection as they strive to create the illusion of the lover's presence as either a spectacle on stage or an image whose qualities can only be wondered at.

Songs and Sonnets

As we have seen, then, the sonnets use theatrical imagery to body forth the emotional situations that they explore. At the same time

Shakespeare's plays have many links with the Sonnets. It is in relatively early plays, especially the comedies believed to have been written around 1593 to 1595, along with the romantic tragedy of *Romeo and Juliet*, that we find the closest links with the Sonnets. No doubt this is in part because, as we have seen, many of them appear to have been written around this time. But it also reflects the fact that in these early plays Shakespeare makes the most use of patterned verse structures. Later, as his styles changed, he developed a freer attitude to versification in which the limitations of the sonnet form would have been less at home. In subject matter too, his plays of the early-to-mid-1590s have more affinities than his later plays with the concerns of the Sonnets, though they never disappear from his work altogether.

Traditionally the form was associated with courtship and wooing. In 'A Lover's Complaint' (discussed in Chapter 8, below) we hear how numerous women in love with the young man addressed to him 'deep-brained sonnets' (l. 209) which they 'weepingly beseeched' (l. 207) him to accept. In Shakespeare's plays, too, wooers sometimes make use of sonnets to further their suits. In *The Two Gentlemen of Verona* Proteus hypocritically advises Thurio, the unwelcome suitor to Silvia, with whom Proteus himself is in love, to 'lay lime to tangle her desires | By wailful sonnets' (3.2.69–70), and obligingly provides a Petrarchan template:

> Say that upon the altar of her beauty
> You sacrifice your tears, your sighs, your heart.
>
> (3.2.72–3)

Happily Thurio has something to hand that, he thinks, will suffice:

> I have a sonnet that will serve the turn
> To give the onset to your good advice.
>
> (3.2.92–3)

In the event he serenades her with the stanzaic song 'Who is Silvia?'—but as the word 'sonnet' could encompass a wide variety of poetic forms, this may even be what he had in mind.

Since, as Abraham Slender's reference to his 'book of songs and sonnets' in *The Merry Wives of Windsor* (see p. 13, above) demonstrates, the terms could be interchangeable, it is just conceivable that

Francis Meres's reference to 'Shakespeare's sugared sonnets among his private friends' could include some of the songs from the plays which Shakespeare originally wrote as poems, with his sonnets, for private circulation. If not, then it is at least possible that some of the Sonnets inspired what eventually became songs in a dramatic context. Some of the songs in Shakespeare's plays and his sonnets share similar or contrasting ideas and images. For example, Sonnet 29's lines

> Haply I think on thee, and then my state
> (Like to the lark at break of day arising)
> From sullen earth sings hymns at heaven's gate;
>
> (ll. 10–12)

are similar to the song that Cloten and his musicians perform to wake the sleeping Innogen in *Cymbeline:* 'Hark, hark the lark at heaven gate sings, | And Phoebus gins arise' (2.3.19–20). Reading the two moments in parallel might encourage more sympathy for the boorish Cloten and place Sonnet 29 at a critical distance by associating its imagined speaker with a self-loathing braggart. Sonnet 97—

> How like a winter hath my absence been
> From thee, the pleasure of the fleeting year?
> What freezings have I felt, what dark days seen?
> What old December's bareness everywhere?
>
> (ll. 1–4)

—is similar in tone and verbal expression to the song Amiens sings in *As You Like It:* 'Blow, blow, thou winter wind . . . Freeze, freeze thou bitter sky' (2.7.175 and 185). The sonnet about the winter of a lover's absence relates to a song sung during banishment from a royal court. Even the 'teeming autumn big with rich increase' is but the 'hope of orphans and unfathered fruit' (Sonnet 97, ll. 6 and 10); 'Most friendship is feigning, most loving mere folly', sings Amiens in Ardenne Forest. Later, two Pages will sing 'It was a lover and his lass' to Touchstone and Audrey, a merry song about the joys of spring and love making (5.3.15–38). Sonnet 98 uses a similar image of spring in a different way:

> When proud-pied April (dressed in all his trim)
> Hath put a spirit of youth in every thing.
>
> (ll. 2–3).

Here, the joys of spring emphasize the absence of the lover; spring in this sonnet is conjured more as a present absence. There are only shadows and 'figures of delight' (l. 11), rather than the immediacy of song. Sweet lovers might love the spring in Ardenne but here it still seems like winter with 'you away' (l. 13). Sonnet 71, 'No longer mourn for me when I am dead', is akin to Feste's song 'Come away, come away death' in *Twelfth Night*. In both poems the speaker is self-indulgently imagining his or her own death without any sympathy or mourning from the lover. 'Do not so much as my poor name rehearse; | But let your love even with my life decay' asks the poetic voice of Sonnet 71 (ll. 11–12), who would rather be forgotten than for the lover to be distressed. Feste's song 'dallies with the innocence of love', according to Orsino (*Twelfth Night*, 2.4.46), and seems to lyricize an exaggerated self-neglect:

> Not a flower, not a flower sweet
>   On my black coffin let there be strewn.
> Not a friend, not a friend greet
>   My poor corpse, where my bones shall be thrown.
>
> (2.4.58–61)

Whether these sonnets were composed before their respective songs seems less important than the connections which can be made between the two and which relate metrically diverse moments in Shakespeare's plays explicitly to his most disciplined poetic form.

The Labours of Love

In *Love's Labour's Lost* whole sonnets are embedded in the dramatic structure as part of the wooing game. Costard intercepts and accidentally gives to Jaquenetta a poem (4.2.106–19) which Biron, who is already weakening in his resolve to abjure the company of women for three years, has sent as a letter to Rosaline. It is written in the form of a sonnet except that each line has six, not five, beats:

> If love make me forsworn, how shall I swear to love?
> Ah, never faith could hold, if not to beauty vowed,
> Though to myself forsworn, to thee I'll faithful prove....
>
> (4.2.106–8)

Read aloud by Nathaniel, it provokes from Holofernes an extraordinary parody of literary criticism: 'Here are only numbers ratified, but for the elegancy, facility, and golden cadence of poetry—*caret*. Ovidius Naso was the man. And why indeed "Naso" but for smelling out the odoriferous flowers of fancy, the jerks of invention?' (4.2.121–5). In the following scene, as Biron's friends, too, weaken in their resolve, they in turn adopt the traditional posture of sonneteers. Love, says Biron, has 'taught me to rhyme and to be melancholy, and here (*showing a paper*) is part of my rhyme, and here (*touching his breast*) my melancholy' (4.3.1–14). The woman he loves, he says, 'hath one o' my sonnets already' (4.3.14–15). This of course is the one that has been intercepted. In the great scene which follows, each of the men in turn reveals his capitulation to Cupid both to the audience and, unwittingly, to his concealed fellows, reading aloud the tributes they have composed for their mistresses. In style they resemble some of the less anguished sonnets of the 1609 volume.

The King reads a poem to the Princess of France written in the form of an extended sonnet—it has an additional couplet at the end. There is surely an element of parody—unconscious on the King's part—in its exaggerations of the conventions of the Petrarchan mode. Each of his despairing tears 'as a coach doth carry thee, | So ridest thou triumphing in my woe' (4.3.32–3). And the added couplet is anticlimactic in its awkward phrasing, jogtrot rhythms, and blatant alliteration:

> O Queen of queens, how far dost thou excel,
> No thought can think nor tongue of mortal tell.
>
> (4.3.38–9)

Next is Longueville's turn; he speaks an entirely regular sonnet (4.3.57–70) attributing his 'false perjury' to 'the heavenly rhetoric' of Maria's eye. Whereas the King had praised his mistress as a queen of queens, Longueville's is a goddess, which serves as a sophistical excuse for his apostasy, since it was women not goddesses that he had forsworn. The last lover to reveal his folly is Dumaine, who offers not a conventional sonnet but an 'ode' (4.3.99–118) written in octosyllabic couplets:

> On a day—alack the day—
> Love, whose month is ever May,
> Spied a blossom passing fair
> Playing in the wanton air...
>
> (4.3.99–102)

Sonnet structures are also in the dialogue of *Love's Labour's Lost*, as at 1.1.80–93, where the form helps to give shape to Biron's reasoning against reading, and three times in the last act (5.2.276–88, 344–57, and 403–16). In the first of these passages the hyperbole of the opening couplet, spoken by Biron, is immediately (and bawdily) parodied by Dumaine in a manner reminiscent of the satire of Petrarchism in Sonnet 130 ('My mistress' eyes'):

BIRON
> O, if the streets were pavèd with thine eyes
>   Her feet were much too dainty for such tread.

DUMAINE
> O vile! Then as she goes, what upward lies
>   The street should see as she walked overhead.
>
> (4.3.276–9)

In *The Comedy of Errors* (3.2.41–54) lines in sonnet form stand as part of a wooing speech. These plays were probably written one after the other, around 1594; clearly the sonnet form was one into which Shakespeare's thoughts fell easily at the time.

As we saw in Chapter 1, extracts from *Love's Labour's Lost* were printed with minor modifications as independent poems in *The Passionate Pilgrim* of 1599, which is attributed as a whole to Shakespeare, with nothing to show that they originated in a play. If nothing else, this shows that the publisher was capitalizing on the popularity of both the sonnet form and Shakespeare's name. Longueville's is the first, which immediately follows the two 'real' sonnets (versions of 138 and 144) that open the volume. It looks at home enough with them. The words 'false perjury' in its opening lines lose in meaning when taken out of their dramatic context, but then many of the Sonnets leave much to the reader's imagination:

> Did not the heavenly rhetoric of thine eye
>   'Gainst whom the world could not hold argument,
> Persuade my heart to this false perjury?
>
> (4.3.57–9)

The 'perjury' is Longueville's breaking of the vow sworn by him and his colleagues that they will have nothing to do with women for the space of three years. *The Passionate Pilgrim* also includes versions of Biron's poem to Rosaline (4.2.106–19) and, in its second part, which has as a separate title 'Sonnets to Sundry Notes of Music', Dumaine's octosyllabic couplets (4.3.99–118); maybe a musical setting of them existed—in Trevor Nunn's National Theatre production of *Love's Labour's Lost* (2003) all the lords' poems in the overhearing scene were sung in a variety of musical styles.

The Shakespeare play that comes closest to the Sonnets in its concern with friendship, with love both unreciprocated and joyfully celebrated, and with the separation of lovers, is *Romeo and Juliet*. It is also the play that makes most extensive and varied use of sonnet form. As we have said, the Prologue to the entire play, and also that to Act 2, are regular sonnets, as if to alert us to the relationship between the form and the play. And the formality of the sonnet structure serves as a way of setting off these choric speeches from the dialogue that surrounds them. Structural features of the plot find a neat parallel in the standard sonnet structure of the opening chorus, directly addressed to the audience, where the first four lines of the quatrain lay out the public theme of family feuding, then the next four sound the note of the ill-fated private love whose tragic resolution will 'bury their parents' strife' (Prologue, l. 8). The first four lines of the sestet are slightly repetitive of the previous four—as if form has dictated content—in their foreshadowing of the tragic ending, but the couplet provides a sense of closure that also looks forward to what is to come:

> The which if you with patient ears attend,
> What here shall miss, our toil shall strive to mend.
>
> (Prologue, ll. 13–14)

Shakespeare uses the sonnet form for a Chorus (usually omitted in performance) to the second act, but after that the device is abandoned. There is, however, a hint of a return to it in the formality and distancing of the Duke's closing of the play in six lines that take the form of the sestet of a sonnet (as do Paris's lines at the tomb, 5.3.12–17). In the meantime the content of a typical sonnet sequence—which Shakespeare's is not—has been echoed in the Petrarchan relationship between Romeo and the unseen, unresponsive Rosaline, and sonnet structure has provided a form for one of the most important pieces of dialogue in the play, the first declaration of love between Romeo and Juliet.

Shakespeare's non-dramatic sonnets are one-voiced poems, many of them to a greater or lesser degree cryptic because we hear only one side of what should be a dialogue—rather like listening to one end of a telephone conversation. Here, however, we have an exquisite dialogue revealing the mutual flowering of young love in an extended sonnet that is both witty and lyrical. It looks forward to the natural consummation of love while also idealizing it, not through a denial of its sexual realization but by consecrating the journey towards that as a pilgrimage which will purge, not create, sin. The dramatic situation is all-important to its effect. The contrast with the immediately preceding violent threats of Tybalt and the inanities of Old Capulet helps, along with stylization of verbal form, to set the lovers' talk off from the bustle of the dance during which it takes place. We enter their private space in a suspension of time which compresses within a couple of minutes of stage time an extent and intensity of experience that would have taken far longer to live through in reality.

> ROMEO (*to Juliet, touching her hand*)
>   If I profane with my unworthiest hand
>   This holiest shrine, the gentler sin is this:
>   My lips, two blushing pilgrims, ready stand
>   To smooth that rough touch with a tender kiss.
> JULIET
>   Good pilgrim, you do wrong your hand too much,
>   Which mannerly devotion shows in this.
>   For saints have hands that pilgrims' hands do touch,
>   And palm to palm is holy palmers' kiss.

ROMEO
> Have not saints lips, and holy palmers, too?

JULIET
> Ay, pilgrim, lips that they must use in prayer.

ROMEO
> O then, dear saint, let lips do what hands do:
> They pray; grant thou, lest faith turn to despair.

JULIET
> Saints do not move, though grant for prayers' sake.

ROMEO
> Then move not while my prayers' effect I take.
>> *He kisses her*

(1.5.92–105)

The dramatic impulse of these lines is enhanced by the delicate comedy with which Juliet unavailingly attempts to insist that pilgrims kiss with hands instead of lips. Their kiss marks the end of the sonnet proper, but it is followed by a coda in the form of an additional quatrain which could be thought of as the opening of another sonnet:

> Thus from my lips, by thine my sin is purged.

JULIET
> Then have my lips the sin that they have took.

ROMEO
> Sin from my lips? O trespass sweetly urged!
> Give me my sin again.
>> *He kisses her*

JULIET
>> You kiss by th' book.

(1.5.106–9)

And then the outer world intrudes as the Nurse calls Juliet away to her mother.

Romeo and Juliet, concerned with 'brawling love' and 'loving hate' (1.1.173), is very consciously a play of extremes. Its romantic attitude to love is counterpointed by extreme bawdy conveyed by both direct statement and innuendo. The same contrast exists in many of Shakespeare's comedies. It is perhaps not too far-fetched to suggest that such paralleling of romantic plot with anti-romantic sub-plot has structural affinities in the Sonnets with their sequence of idealizing poems addressed to a male followed by more cynical poems addressed to a female. With all the play's self-conscious identification with the sonnet form, it is suggestive that Juliet herself is not quite 14 years old (1.3.19, etc.) She may share a sonnet with Romeo, but her life, cut off in her youth, does not quite add up and equate to the number of lines most commonly required in a Shakespearian sonnet of love.

Shakespeare makes use of the sonnet form less frequently in later plays. In *As You Like It*, predictably, the verses addressed to 'the fair, the chaste, and unexpressive she' which Orlando fixes to a tree are a sonnet, albeit a foreshortened one (3.2.1–10), though the poems he writes are not. In *All's Well That Ends Well* the form sets off the letter (read by Reynaldo) written by Helen to the Countess (3.4.4–17). In *Henry V* it gives a distancing effect—rather like that created by the final lines of *Romeo and Juliet*—to the Epilogue. In *Pericles*, the magical appearance of Diana is heightened by her speaking a shortened sonnet as she descends from the heavens (Sc. 21.225–34), and, in extended form, the sonnet makes a final return late in Shakespeare's career in the resounding lines spoken in similar circumstances by Jupiter in *Cymbeline* (5.5.187–207). *All is True (Henry VIII)* has a sonnet in rhyming couplets as an epilogue.

'My Very Deed of Love'[2]

The ideas and themes found in the Sonnets, as well as their poetic form, can be discerned in many of Shakespeare's plays. To trace and discuss all the affinities that exist between the 1609 Quarto and the plays would require a book-length study. We can attempt only a sketch of the most prominent.

Significance has sometimes been attached to the fact that, just as there is at least one 'dark' woman in the Sonnets, so there are a number of them in the plays. This might well seem merely curious except that some of them occur in contexts compellingly reminiscent of the Sonnets. In *Love's Labour's Lost*, the sonnet play (along with *Romeo and Juliet*) *par excellence*, the King tells Biron 'Thy love [that is, Rosaline] is black as ebony.' Biron takes up the idea in sonnet-like verses expressing paradoxes resembling those of some of the Sonnets:

> Is ebony like her? O word divine!
> A wife of such wood were felicity.

> O, who can give an oath? Where is a book,
>   That I may swear beauty doth beauty lack
> If that she learn not of her eye to look?
>   No face is fair that is not full so black.
>
>   (4.3.246–51)

'That I may swear beauty doth beauty lack' is close indeed to 'Then will I swear beauty herself is black', in Sonnet 132 (l. 13), and similar wordplay is to be found in Sonnets 127 ('now is black beauty's successive heir', l. 3) and 131 ('Thy black is fairest in my judgement's place', l. 12).

The presentation in *Romeo and Juliet* of the classic Petrarchan (but not Shakespearian) sonnet situation of the lover wooing a marble-hearted mistress is incomplete in that we never see Rosaline (to whom, intriguingly, Shakespeare gives the same name as Biron's mistress). There is, however, a fuller, gently comic version of the situation in *As You Like It*, in the desperation of Silvius's love for Phoebe, who, according to Rosalind (that name again! But here it derives from the source, Thomas Lodge's novel *Rosalynde*), has 'inky brows', black silk hair', and 'bugle eyeballs' (bugles were beads, often coloured black). Her lofty attitude towards him is sharply punctured by Rosalind's realism: 'down on your knees | And thank heaven, fasting, for a good man's love' (3.5.58–9). Far closer to the stormy relationship between the poet of the Sonnets and his dark woman is that between Mark Antony and Cleopatra, who is 'with Phoebus' amorous pinches black' (*Antony and Cleopatra*, 1.5.28). Like the poet, Antony seeks in vain to break off from his 'enchanting queen' (1.2.121).

The other sort of relationship adumbrated in the Sonnets and dramatized in plays is that between two men. In the poems it is an unequal relationship. In the first seventeen the poet is in the position of an adviser, and in others he writes directly of being older than his friends. There is a sense that the emotional commitment is greater on the poet's side than on the friends'. Certainly the poetic voice seems vulnerable, easily hurt. The relationship is discussed in terms not simply of friendship but of love. The intensity of the passion as, for instance, he answers his own question

> What's new to speak, what now to register,
> That may express my love, or thy dear merit?

cannot but suggest physical desire in its statement of mutual possession:

> Nothing, sweet boy; but yet, like prayers divine,
> I must each day say o'er the very same,
> Counting no old thing old, thou mine, I thine,
> Even as when first I hallowed thy fair name.
>
> (Sonnet 108, ll. 3–8)

The phrase 'sweet boy' (l. 5) can, as Burrow remarks in his note, 'carry
homoerotic overtones, as when Richard Barnfield, *Cynthia* 14.5, calls
his Ganymede-like male lover "sweet boy" . . . These associations may
have prompted Benson to one of his bowdlerizations, "sweet-love." '
And though 'hallowed' may (as Burrow implies, with a reference to the
Lord's Prayer) mean 'sanctified', it may also take on the sense of
'hallooed', as in Viola's 'Halloo your name to the reverberate hills'
(*Twelfth Night*, 1.5.261).

Inevitably Shakespeare's plays frequently portray friendship. Male
friends often speak of their relationship in an uninhibited fashion that
might be taken for the language of lovers. In the first two speeches of
The Two Gentlemen of Verona, for instance, Valentine addresses 'my
loving Proteus' (1.1.1), who replies 'sweet Valentine' (1.1.11). There is,
however, nothing to indicate that their friendship has anything physical about it. But in a few plays male friendship is portrayed with an
intensity comparable to that shown in the Sonnets. Perhaps the most
conspicuous example is that between Antonio and Bassanio in *The
Merchant of Venice*, written around 1596 or 1597. The men's respective
ages are not directly stated, but Antonio, a melancholic, is an established businessman who takes a protective interest in Bassanio, who is
clearly young. In performance it is common to play Antonio as older,
sometimes considerably older, than his friend. Other characters
within the play see their friendship as exceptional. Salerio, reporting
on their parting after Bassanio has left to pursue his wooing of Portia
in Belmont, says of Antonio

> And even there, his eye being big with tears,
> Turning his face, he put his hand behind him
> And, with affection wondrous sensible,
> He wrung Bassanio's hand; and so they parted.

To which Solanio replies:

> I think he only loves the world for him.
>
> (2.8.46–50)

Somewhat similar is the friendship between another Antonio, the Sea Captain, and the young Sebastian, in *Twelfth Night*, written around 1600. The identity of name is curious, as if it might have had some special significance for Shakespeare. This Antonio, too, is reasonably portrayed in performance as considerably older than his friend. Like the poet in the Sonnets, who is at times 'in disgrace with fortune and men's eyes' (Sonnet 29, l. 1), Antonio feels himself oppressed by 'the malignancy of my fate' (*Twelfth Night*, 2.1.4). And he too feels intense passion for his friend.

> I have many enemies in Orsino's court,
> Else would I very shortly see thee there.

But then love overcomes his fear:

> But come what may, I do adore thee so
> That danger shall seem sport, and I will go.
>
> (2.1.40–3)

The intensity of love is such that at the very thought of it, as in Sonnet 30, 'All losses are restored, and sorrows end.' Antonio's rhyming couplet is similar, too, to that repeated in Sonnets 36 and 96:

> But do not so; I love thee in such sort
> As thou being mine, mine is thy good report.
>
> (Sonnets 36 and 96, ll. 13–14)

Whatever damage might be done to this speaker's reputation, whatever danger might ensue, loyalty to the loved one remains the single, most important motivation. Later Antonio will speak of his 'desire' which, 'More sharp than filèd steel, did spur me forth' (*Twelfth Night*, 3.3.4–5). It is unsurprising that the relationship between both these Antonios and their friends has, like that between poet and friend in the Sonnets, been interpreted as one that goes beyond friendship to love in the fullest sense of the word.

The persuasion to procreate in Sonnets 1–17 has verbal resonance with *Twelfth Night*. On first representing Orsino's suit to Olivia, Viola talks in prose until the moment when she is granted a closer look at Olivia, who privately removes her veil. Viola breaks into verse on seeing Olivia's beauty, and her words resound with the Sonnets' argument to love and procreate so as to ensure the survival of one's beauty:

> 'Tis beauty truly blent, whose red and white
> Nature's own sweet and cunning hand laid on.
> Lady, you are the cruell'st she alive
> If you will lead these graces to the grave
> And leave the world no copy.
>
> (*Twelfth Night*, 1.5.228–32)

In Sonnet 11, the poet implores in almost exactly the same way:

> Let those whom Nature hath not made for store,
> Harsh, featureless, and rude, barrenly perish.
> Look whom she best endowed she gave the more,
> Which bounteous gift thou shouldst in bounty cherish.
> She carved thee for her seal, and meant thereby
> Thou shouldst print more, not let that copy die.
>
> (ll. 9–14)

Twelfth Night also dramatizes Sonnet 20's 'master mistress' in the figure of Viola disguised as the page Cesario being equally attractive to Duke Orsino and the Countess Olivia. The stage image of the disguised Viola being desired by both her master and her mistress in Act 5 Scene 1 relates closely to the lover being described in the Sonnet:

> OLIVIA
>   Where goes Cesario?
> VIOLA
>   After him I love
> More than I love these eyes, more than my life,
> More by all mores than e'er I shall love wife.
>
> (5.1.132–4)

These words might be understood to refer to an explicitly passionate relationship and come from the mouth of someone who appears to be a young man. Sonnet 20 describes a similar effect. Viola's appearance in some way also seduces Olivia, whether intentionally or not. She is guilty of 'Gilding the object whereupon [she] gazeth' as she 'steals men's eyes and women's souls amazeth' (Sonnet 20, ll. 6, 8). The reunion of the twins Viola and Sebastian and the revelation of Viola's true identity show the impossibility of Olivia being 'betrothed both to a maid and man' (*Twelfth Night*, 5.1.261); Orsino's steps towards self-restoration and the definition of what might in a production be portrayed as his own deeply unsettling desire, include the definition of Viola now being her 'master's mistress'. He has yet to discover, after she has changed into her female clothes, whether Viola as a woman will be as attractive to him as Viola as a boy. Olivia, wearing black and mourning the death of her brother, might be a further, imagined candidate for the dark mistress and is verbally attacked by Orsino. His twelve-line speech of blank verse, if separated from its dramatic context, becomes a poem in mood and tone not dissimilar to one of the later sonnets.

> Why should I not, had I the heart to do it,
> Like to th'Egyptian thief, at point of death
> Kill what I love—a savage jealousy
> That sometime savours nobly. But hear me this:
> Since you to non-regardance cast my faith,
> And that I partly know the instrument
> That screws me from my true place in your favour,
> Live you the marble-breasted tyrant still.
> But this your minion, whom I know you love,
> And whom, by heaven I swear, I tender dearly,
> Him will I tear out of that cruel eye
> Where he sits crownèd in his master's spite.
>
> (5.1.115–26)

Orsino's speech ends with a rhyming couplet comparing Olivia to a raven, and attacking her as a sonnet-like black-hearted lady:

> I'll sacrifice the lamb that I do love
> To spite a raven's heart within a dove.
>
> (5.1.128–9)

Shakespeare's Sketchbook

Most great artists such as Michelangelo, da Vinci, Rembrandt, and Turner use sketchbooks; for Shakespeare the writing of sonnets might in some ways have served a comparable purpose. When read alongside the plays, the Sonnets can soon seem like a collection of fourteen-line monologues, compressed character studies which, in the plays, are given fuller dramatic development. The first quatrain of Sonnet 19 might be part of one of Lear's great curses:

> Devouring Time, blunt thou the lion's paws,
> And make the earth devour her own sweet brood,
> Pluck the keen teeth from the fierce tiger's jaws,
> And burn the long-lived phoenix in her blood....

Sonnets 33 and 34 use similar imagery to Hal's soliloquy, who permits 'the basest clouds to ride | With ugly rack on his celestial face' (Sonnet 33, ll. 5–6), 'To smother up his beauty from the world' before 'Redeeming time' (*1 Henry IV*, 1.2.196, 214) and ransoming 'all ill deeds' (Sonnet 34, l. 14). Sonnet 40 might be Antony speaking to Cleopatra: 'Take all my loves, my love, yea, take them all' (l. 1); Sonnet 138 might be Antony talking about her at his highest point of disillusionment: 'When my love swears that she is made of truth, | I do believe her though I know she lies' (ll. 1–2). Sonnets 46 and 47, in describing the relationship between what the eye sees and what the heart feels, might be related to *A Midsummer Night's Dream*. The speaker in Sonnet 47 is 'famished for a look' (l. 3) like Helena for her Demetrius; Sonnet 75 engages with similar ideas of affection as sustenance: 'And by and by clean starvèd for a look' (l. 10). This self-abasing speaker could again be Helena speaking to Demetrius, or Helen speaking to Bertram in *All's Well That Ends Well*. Sonnet 48 might be about Troilus articulating the absolutist nature of his love for Cressida and contrasting fidelity with falsity, evoking comparisons with theft as Cressida herself is 'left the prey of every vulgar thief' in the Greek camp (l. 8). The poetic voice of Sonnet 57 might be Kate finding out how to play another love game with Petruccio: 'Being your slave, what should I do but tend | Upon the hours and times of your desire?' (ll. 1–2). Sonnet 62 might be penned by an imaginary Malvolio or Richard III: 'Sin of self-love possesseth all mine eye' (l. 1). It even evokes an imaginary Richard II, as the speaker peers into a looking-glass at line 9 and learns from what he sees. Sonnet 85 could be a self-vindication by Cordelia, thinking 'good thoughts, whilst other write good words' (l. 5). Cordelia, whose love is 'more ponderous than [her] tongue' (*The Tragedy of King Lear*, 1.1.78), could also easily speak Sonnet 85's couplet:

> Then others for the breath of words respect;
> Me for my dumb thoughts, speaking in effect.
>
> (ll. 13–14)

Sonnet 92 could be spoken by Othello to Desdemona. It conveys a similar, fatalistic trust and a sinister underlying threat and vulnerability:

> And life no longer than thy love will stay,
> For it depends upon that love of thine.
>
> . . . . . .
>
> Thou canst not vex me with inconstant mind,
> Since that my life on thy revolt doth lie.
> O, what a happy title do I find,
> Happy to have thy love, happy to die!
> But what's so blessèd fair that fears no blot?
> Thou mayst be false, and yet I know it not.
>
> (ll. 3–4 and 9–14).

On his being reunited with Desdemona on Cyprus, Othello describes similar feelings:

> If it were now to die
> 'Twere now to be most happy, for I fear
> My soul hath her content so absolute
> That not another comfort like to this
> Succeeds in unknown fate
>
> (*Othello*, 2.1.190–4)

Sonnet 121 might be spoken by Iago, ''Tis better to be vile than vile esteemed' (l.1) and contains an echo of his negation of knowable subjectivity—'I am not what I am' (1.1.65, a negation he also oddly shares with Viola: *Twelfth Night*, 3.2.139). Sonnet 121 rather presents an illusion of a knowable and divine-like sense of selfhood: 'I am that I am' (l.9; Exodus 3: 14). Like Iago, though, the speaker of Sonnet 121 is slippery and recognizes that moral absolutes are made as much by 'others' seeing', as by one's own feelings. 'I may be straight though they themselves be bevel' (l.11) provides a way into the kind of psychopathic nature that Shakespeare explores so fully in Iago. Sonnet 114 might be a private meditation by Gertrude, thinking about how she herself is drawn to the poison in Claudius, as well as tragically to the poisoned chalice in the final scene. Sonnet 122 is all about memory and is, we are reliably informed by a friend of ours who knows all the sonnets by heart, the hardest one to commit to memory. It could be Hamlet trying to remember the Ghost's words and injunctions: 'To keep an adjunct to remember thee | Were to import forgetfulness in me' (Sonnet 122, ll. 13–14). Sonnet 129 might be an inner and tumultuous meditation by Angelo, full of self-disgust and terrified of his own sexuality, leading him to a hell of his own making, despite his self-righteous sounding name. Sonnet 140 could be either Hamlet talking to Ophelia or Ophelia talking to Hamlet; it might be an imagined letter exchanged between the two of them:

> For if I should despair I should grow mad,
> And in my madness might speak ill of thee.
> Now this ill-wresting world is grown so bad,
> Mad slanders by mad ears believèd be.
>
> (ll. 9–12)

Sonnet 141 might be Orlando talking to the disguised Rosalind: 'In faith, I do not love thee with mine eyes' and accepting that his love for Rosalind which 'makes me sin awards me pain' (ll. 1 and 14). Since he is having to pretend that Ganymede is Rosalind herself, he might feel torn when he finds himself desiring a young man; possibly desiring, in short, too much of a good thing.

As well as being sketchbooks for characterizations, or character studies in miniature, the Sonnets also contain occasional lines which can take the reader to a comparable moment in the plays themselves. So, for instance, 'But from thine eyes my knowledge I derive' (Sonnet 14, l. 9) is comparable to Biron's 'From women's eyes this doctrine I derive', the culmination of his great and comic vindication of love in *Love's Labour's Lost* (4.3.326). *The Tragedy of King Lear* can be connected to Sonnets 83 and 116: 'How far a modern quill doth come too short' (Sonnet 83, l. 7) is rather like Regan criticizing Goneril, that 'she comes too short' (*The Tragedy of King Lear*, 1.1.72) in her speech of love to Lear. Incidentally, if read out of context, and put together to form a single speech of fifteen lines, Goneril and Regan's love claims can be reimagined as the poetic voice of a love sonnet (1.1.55–61 and 69–76). Sonnet 116 with the (ironic?) surety it seeks amongst the fragile certainties of love might be read satirically against the aged King Lear whose mind does admit great impediments, who does alter love when he alteration finds, who does look on tempests and is shaken, who is indeed time's fool, and peers over the edge of doom. With Lear in mind the poetic voice of Sonnet 116 certainly commits great error by the time the reader arrives at the rhyming couplet which serves rather to undercut any notion of love, than to affirm it:

> If this be error and upon me proved,
> I never writ, nor no man ever loved.
>
> (ll. 13–14)

So Shakespeare's sonnets explore theatrical expression in themselves; they can be related to the songs in the plays as well as seek identification with a comparable use of poetic form, content, ideas, and verbal expression. To return, finally, to *Twelfth Night*, when Viola describes how she would woo Olivia if she were in love with her, she says that she would 'Halloo your name to the reverberate hills'. In Sonnet 108 (as we have seen) the poetic voice recalls the first time she/he 'hallowed thy fair name' (l. 8). Both Shakespeare's sonnet collection and his plays seem to cry out to be mapped together over a similar landscape of meaning and expression. And perhaps those sonnets that are not readily related to the drama contain the seeds of scenes and speeches in plays that Shakespeare never got round to writing.

The Place of
'A Lover's Complaint'

At the end of Shakespeare's collection of sonnets in the 1609 Quarto is printed a 329-line poem called 'A Lover's Complaint'. It has a separate heading repeating the attribution to Shakespeare, but in spite of this its authorship has long been questioned. Estimates vary as to the number of new words the poem contains which are not found any-where in Shakespeare. Colin Burrow (p. 139) counts forty-nine, for example 'plaintful' (l. 2), 'fluxive' (l. 50), and 'pensived' (l. 219). In an article for *Shakespeare Quarterly*, 48/2 (1997), Ward Elliott counts eighty-eight new words and continues seriously to doubt the poem's attribution to Shakespeare. Critics have long found the poem awk-ward and difficult in both style and content. Kenneth Muir and MacDonald P. Jackson both argued strongly for the poem's authenti-city in the 1960s,[1] and for a while the matter seemed to be settled, but in recent years scholars have rearticulated doubts about the attribu-tion. Brian Vickers thoroughly signalled his doubt in *Counterfeiting Shakespeare* (2002), and implausibly suggested Sir John Davies as the author in an article for the *Times Literary Supplement* (5 December 2003). Any theory about authorship alternative to Shakespeare's own, however, has to explain away the printing of 'William Shakespeare' after the poem's title and the fact that it was published in the same quarto volume of 1609 along with the Sonnets themselves.

We are interested in the poem precisely because of its appearing at the same time and in the same volume as the Sonnets. The date of 'A Lover's Complaint' is difficult to determine and scholars have

_____ Woe is me! too early I attended a youthful Suit.

E. Edwards del.

J. Hall sculp.

Fig. 10. This first known illustration of 'A Lover's Complaint' comes from the 1774 volume of *Poems* included in John Bell's multi-volume edition of the complete works. In it the Sonnets are reprinted from Benson's corrupt edition of 1640.

placed it between 1599 and 1609; John Kerrigan suggests 1602–5. Stylometric evidence allows for the possibility that Shakespeare might have written it while he was putting his sonnets together and ordering them. If so, it could be regarded as his own (or someone else's) creative response to his collection. Though in the past the Sonnets were often published without it, recent editions have tended to include 'A Lover's Complaint' to convey the impression of their being 'mutually illuminating' (Kerrigan, p. 14), 'a final meditation on sexual desire and its consequences, which sits questioningly beside the sonnet form' (Burrow, p. 40). Whether it is by Shakespeare or not (and the two authors of this book represent both conviction and uncertainty on this point) we would like to consider it as a work which is both enriched by being read alongside the Sonnets and which enriches a reading of the Sonnets, as well as offering points of comparison with Shakespeare's other work.

There are strains of *Twelfth Night* (the young man's beauty, like Viola/Cesario's, is described as feminine, *Twelfth Night*, 1.4.31–4; 'Lover's Complaint', ll. 92–100); *Othello* (Desdemona's song of willow is a similar kind of complaint); *Hamlet* (Ophelia sings complaints in her madness); *Measure for Measure* (there is mention of a nun whom the young man of 'A Lover's Complaint' has seduced at l. 260); *All's Well That Ends Well* (the caddish behaviour of the young man makes him more like Bertram than any other Shakespearian role); *Troilus and Cressida* (the maid might be described as 'fickle', l. 5, but seems as absolutist in her resolve and passion as Troilus, whereas the young man of the poem is unfaithful, which makes him more like Cressida); *King Lear* (the young man displays selfish emotion; the woman is seeking certainties in love); and *Cymbeline* (there are several verbal echoes, for example 'gyves', l. 242, and 'aptness', l. 306, which suggest a late date for the poem since *Cymbeline* can be dated between 1610 and 1611).

Especially popular in the late sixteenth century, a poetic complaint was historically a lament, a confrontation, and an argument, usually made by someone of high status; but this is not an absolute rule, nor do complaints have to be only about love. In the influential and frequently revised *A Mirror for Magistrates* (first published 1559), the ghosts of historical figures who came to a bad end tell their sad stories. Though most complaints are voiced by men, John Kerrigan has compiled an anthology, *Motives of Woe: Shakespeare and Female Complaint* (Oxford, 1991), centring on Shakespeare, of women's complaints from Chaucer to Alexander Pope.

It was not unusual for sonnets to be followed by longer poems. Late sixteenth-century readers developed a taste for them and would not have been surprised to find complaints at the end of sonnet collections. Samuel Daniel's *Delia* is followed by *The Complaint of Rosamund* (1592), Thomas Lodge's *Phillis* is followed by *The Complaint of Elstred* (1593), Richard Barnfield's *Cassandra* succeeds *Cynthia, with Certain Sonnets* (1595). 'A Lover's Complaint' tells of a young woman who has been deceived by an inconstant young man. Shakespeare's narrator (whose gender is never revealed) overhears the distress and laments of a 'fickle maid full pale' (l. 5), echoing from a pastoral valley, a 'sad-tuned tale' (l. 4) which the maid tells to a dubiously 'reverend man . . . a blusterer' (ll. 57–8). It emerges she has been forsaken in love by a young man who is described in terms of universal adoration and who gives her tokens of his other lovers, before convincing her of his own unhappiness and leaving her to hers. Like *The Rape of Lucrece*, 'A Lover's Complaint' is written in rhyme-royal, seven-lined stanzas, rhyming ababbcc, which allows for an intense effect of interiority, with the repeated rhyme of one sound three times as well as a rhyming couplet at the end of the stanza (for example, 'yielded', 'shielded', 'builded'; 'foil' and 'spoil', ll. 149, 151–4).

The Lover of Shakespeare's title could be either the 'fickle maid full pale' whom the narrator overhears and who speaks most of the poem, or the disdainful, superior young man who has rejected her, and whose apparent unhappiness she recounts, as well as her own. The initial appearance of the narrator provides the effect of a framing device which, like that involving Christopher Sly in *The Taming of the Shrew*, is absorbed by the main action and disappears. The poem begins with an echo: an original voice has become something strange to be related afresh. 'A Lover's Complaint', like the Sonnets, offers the reader multiple perspectives which they must explore for themselves. The narrator is at two removes from the maid's account: it is 'A plaintful story from a sist'ring vale' (l. 2) which she tells to someone else, but which is mysteriously reborn by the 'hill whose concave womb reworded' (l. 1) the 'double voice' (l. 3) to which the narrator attends. As an echoed tale, 'A Lover's Complaint' upsets any notion of a reliable poetic authority for the events which subsequently unfold. Despite the maid's 'suffering ecstasy' (l. 69), she manages to recount her experience to a passing cattle grazer. Like the lover who has left her, this old man it seems has broken several hearts in his time, too: 'Sometime a blusterer that the ruffle knew | Of court, city' (ll. 58–9). There is, too, the beautiful young man who has forsaken her (described from l. 79) and the 'nun | Or sister sanctified' he speaks of (a woman who has pledged chastity, if not taken up Holy Orders) whose heart he has also broken (ll. 232–66). When the poem is considered as a creative appendage to the Sonnets, its enigmatic quality raises many questions and possible points of connection which allow its readers to reflect on the resounding echo which the Sonnets themselves leave in their wake, tugging at the reader's memory.

In seeking to relate the personalities in the Sonnets to those in 'A Lover's Complaint', there can be no direct lines of correspondence. Sasha Roberts overstates the contrast between the 'claustrophobic misogyny' of the Sonnets, in their vilification of the mistress, and the portrayal of 'male sexual duplicity' in 'A Lover's Complaint'.[2] Reading intertextually in this way can make the Sonnets and 'A Lover's Complaint' seem like both sides of the same coin. In the end, especially if the authorship of 'A Lover's Complaint' is not settled, they must remain separate entities whose intertextual association is nevertheless richly rewarding. The emotionally involved poet persona of the Sonnets might be transformed into the disinterested, framed narrator who remains silent after the beginning of the complaint and allows the reader to guess how much has been learned, if anything. But the fluid 'I' of the Sonnets is also recognizable in the destructive and passionate voices of the young woman and the young man. Oscar Wilde noticed this, quoting lines from 'A Lover's Complaint' in *The Portrait of Mr W. H.* and writing 'It had never been pointed out before that the shepherd of this lovely pastoral, whose "youth in art and art in youth" are described with such subtlety of phrase and passion, was none other than the Mr W H of the Sonnets' (Wilde, ed. Holland, pp. 38–9).

Similarly, the abused and adulterous mistress of the Sonnets can find her parallel in both the distress of the young woman and the sexually careless young man: 'errors of the blood, none of the mind'

(l. 184). Katherine Duncan-Jones suggests a sexual 'balance' in which the misogynistic tone of the later sonnets is counterpoised here by 'the sympathetic presentation of a nameless maid' (Duncan-Jones, p. 88). If one can identify two triangular relationships in some of the Sonnets (Nos. 78–80, 82–6, and 131–6), then here it is as if the reader is faced with a triangle which is forever adjusting its three points of referral. Even a woman associated with black is involved in the figure of the nun ('All vows and consecration giving place', l. 263) whose thwarted relationship with the young man provides a total inversion of Angelo and Isabella in *Measure for Measure*.

It is possible, then, to consider 'A Lover's Complaint' as providing the reader with a context in which to reflect upon some of the concerns and moods articulated in the Sonnets, as well as an invitation critically and creatively to reappraise the earlier poems. There is a fresh start with the wanton destruction of love tokens. Echoing the tempests on Lear's heath and the final song of *Twelfth Night*, the maiden is possessed by the

> Tearing of papers, breaking rings a-twain,
> Storming her world with sorrow's wind and rain.
>
> (ll. 6–7)

Her handkerchief, moistened by her tears, contains an embroidered text of 'conceited characters' (l. 16), and later Shakespeare describes the 'folded schedules . . . Which she perused, sighed, tore, and gave the flood' (ll. 43–4). There are, too, even more intimate papers written in blood which become reminders of Shakespeare's sonnets with her line: 'Ink would have seemed more black and damnèd here' (l. 54; Sonnet 63, 13–14, for one example). We learn later that these include 'deep-brained sonnets' (l. 209) which the youth received from his admirers and which he passed on to her (ll. 221–2) before stealing her virginity (l. 297). These papers

> in top of rage the lines she rents,
> Big discontent so breaking their contents
>
> (ll. 55–6)

In the poetic and printed reality of the 1609 Quarto, might not these papers and schedules be, or at least represent, Shakespeare's own sonnets that the reader has just finished reading? In such close emotional and literary proximity, such destruction of a 'register of lies' (l. 52) undercuts any notion of truth in love poetry, and especially Shakespeare's own.

Similarly, in relation to the theatrical metaphor and awareness that runs through the Sonnets, the youth in 'A Lover's Complaint' possesses many attributes that one associates with an actor:

> So on the tip of his subduing tongue
> All kind of arguments and question deep,
> All replication prompt and reason strong,
> For his advantage still did wake and sleep.
> To make the weeper laugh, the laugher weep,
> He had the dialect and different skill,
> Catching all passions in his craft of will.
>
> (ll. 120–6)

The line endings themselves create a powerful picture of his seductive capability: his 'strong' 'tongue' with emphatic 'skill' and 'will', making his unfortunate lovers 'weep' 'deep' in their 'sleep'. He has been admired by many 'that never touched his hand' (l. 141) and who 'dialogued for him' (l. 132), imagining his speeches of love. His portraiture is the prize of many (l. 134) and his performative skill masks his 'all-hurting aim' (l. 310) with 'the garment of a grace' (l. 316). Here is an arch-deceiver whose exploits themselves are 'a double voice accorded' (l. 3): he is two-faced. This duality of truth and seeming is present in the androgyny of the youth's appearance, like the 'master-mistress' of Sonnet 20. 'Small show of man was yet upon his chin' (l. 92), 'maiden-tongued he was, and thereof free' (l. 100), 'That he did in the general bosom reign | Of young, of old, and sexes both enchanted' (ll. 127–8). He is a potently desirable and potently destructive figure of universal appeal.

In relating the poem further to the universality of sexual desire expressed through the Sonnets in their shifts between male and/or female addressees, it is useful to consider the work of two twentieth-century writers: one a Shakespearian critic, the other a creative genius. G. Wilson Knight writes at length, albeit anachronistically, about 'bisexual integration' in the Sonnets. For Knight, 'the creative consciousness is bisexual; otherwise there could be no creation; and in representing the poet's engagement with both sexes, the Sonnets describe steps on the path towards the creative integration'.[3] The pathway of the Sonnets leads to 'A Lover's Complaint'—at least it did in 1609 and does today in four editions: Wells, Kerrigan, Duncan-Jones, and Burrow. Virginia Woolf appropriates Samuel Taylor Coleridge to expound similar remarks in chapter 6 of *A Room of One's Own*. Through reflecting that a purely masculine or feminine mind is unable to create fully, she considers that:

[Coleridge] meant, perhaps, that the androgynous mind is resonant and porous; that it transmits emotion without impediment; that it is naturally creative, incandescent and undivided. In fact one goes back to Shakespeare's mind as the type of androgynous, of the man-womanly mind.

Although, unlike Knight, she does not specifically address the Sonnets, her language here resonates with Sonnet 116. Her ideally androgynous creative consciousness, like Shakespeare's 'marriage of true minds' (Sonnet 116, l. 1), 'transmits emotion without impediment'. Appearing and being read alongside the Sonnets, 'A Lover's Complaint' echoes and develops their major points of focus and completes the 1609 Quarto by making it a pansexual experience for the reader. If the gender of Shakespeare's addressees can be understood to be in constant flux (see Table 1), then the non-gendered narratival voice of 'A Lover's Complaint' seems to reconsider the potentially destructive quality of androgyny through the figure of a universally adored, but locally lamented youth.

Other echoes of the Sonnets in 'A Lover's Complaint' include a reference to the woman's appearance:

> The carcass of a beauty spent and done:
> Time had not scythèd all that youth begun,
>
> (ll. 11–12).

Time's inevitable scythe is approaching, ready for the harvest; the woman has had sex, but not yet, as far we know, procreated (Sonnet 12, l. 13), thus indicating she is a victim of Time, rather than a challenger. If Sonnet 126 mentions Time's 'audit', here the audit is of precious love tokens which the youth has collected (l. 230). Sonnet 31, line 10 fondly remembers 'trophies' of past lovers dead in the image of the beloved; here 'trophies of affections hot' (l. 218) again refers to the gifts the young man has acquired from those who have adored him and whom he has disappointed. His command to the young woman to 'Take all these similes' (l. 227, presumably a reference to the sonnets he is giving to her) recalls the passionate beginning of Sonnet 40: 'Take all my loves, my love, yea, take them all'. The young man in 'A Lover's Complaint' does not understand the meaning of the word 'love', and can only traffic comparisons to it on paper. Like the poetic voice of Sonnet 40, and that which is later betrayed by the mistress, the young woman knows she is being deceived in love but cannot escape the damage this entails:

> O father, what a hell of witchcraft lies
> In the small orb of one particular tear?
>
> (ll. 288–9)

Sonnet 153 explains 'Where Cupid got new fire: my mistress' eyes' (l. 14) and Sonnet 154 that 'Love's fire heats water; water cools not love' (l. 14). Coming at the end of the collection, it is as if they serve to introduce the pain and distress that love causes in 'A Lover's Complaint'. Here the young woman complains that her tears are inspired afresh by her recollections of the young man. His remembered tears of persuasion are like 'a hell' for her, where 'Love's fire' never goes out.

'A Lover's Complaint' offers a creative and antithetical response to the Sonnets and an emphatic reminder that love might at its most heartfelt be no more than lies after all, told in order to fulfil a purely selfish desire. Katherine Duncan-Jones describes the cumulative effect as 'a book of lies and lying' from which there is no escape (p. 95). Those who forget, or choose not to notice this, the poem warns us, are likely to be deeply wounded. The relationship described in Sonnet 138 has found a way of coping with and accepting the lies told in love, by forgetting them through the power of sex: 'When my love swears that she is made of truth, | I do believe her though I know she lies' (ll. 1–2). No such possibility exists for the two lovers trapped in this complaint which seeks to deny closure. Will the maid tell her story again to someone else when she moves on? At best, the reader might be reminded of the initial narrator, an inconsistent presence, overhearing the woman's distracted tale told in a valley, at one remove on the top of a lonely hillside.

Part II

The Later Publication of the Sonnets

Absence of the Sonnets, along with Shakespeare's other poems, from the first collected edition of Shakespeare need imply no disrespect. The title of the First Folio of 1623—*Mr William Shakespeare's Comedies, Histories and Tragedies*—explicitly limits its contents to plays. It was put together by Shakespeare's theatrical colleagues, Heminges and Condell; even if they wished to reprint the poems, practical problems may have deterred them. The narrative poems were still selling successfully, so their copyright holders would have had no incentive to release them. The Sonnets, on the other hand, appear not to have sold well. No second edition appeared, and the survival of at least thirteen copies shows that the first printing was not read to pieces. So far as we know, Thomas Thorpe still held the copyright. He may well not have wished to jeopardize the sale of any remaining copies by making them available elsewhere.

Some of the sonnets continued to circulate privately. Versions are found in a number of manuscripts dating from around 1620 onwards, some in adaptation for setting to music; their compilers may have copied them from the 1609 edition, or even possibly from earlier manuscripts such as those from which the versions in *The Passionate Pilgrim* derived, which may have been in Shakespeare's hand. Five manuscripts of Sonnet 2 ('When forty winters...'), now usually taken as addressed to a man, bear the title 'To one that Would die a Maid', other manuscripts call it *Spes Altera* ('another hope'), and one has the heading 'A Lover to his Mistress'. Burrow reprints the poem with collations from the various manuscripts, and discusses the possibility that it may be an early draft of the poem as printed in 1609.

Although the absence of the Sonnets (and other poems) from the First Folio may have been involuntary, it had a long-lasting effect on Shakespeare's reputation as a non-dramatic poet. The Folio was reprinted in 1632, 1663, and 1685, always without the poems even though the second issue (1664) of the Third Folio added *Pericles* and six apocryphal plays. The narrative poems continued to be reprinted independently, but they were set aside from the main body of Shakespeare's work, and the Sonnets were even more firmly marginalized.

It was not until the appearance of the publisher John Benson's *Poems Written by William Shakespeare*, printed in 1639 but dated 1640, that most, but not all, of the sonnets reappeared in print. This is a deliberately fraudulent volume, carefully designed to pull the wool over the eyes of the officials of the Stationers' Company, who guarded copyright. Benson disguises the sonnets by altering their order; he omits eight of them; he runs some of them together as if they were a single poem; he gives them banal titles such as 'An Invitation to Marriage' (for an amalgam of poems from the opening sequence), 'Love's Relief' (an amalgamation of Nos. 33 to 35), 'The Picture of True Love' (No. 116), 'Self-Flattery of her Beauty' (Nos. 113–15); and he alters pronouns and terms of address from male to female in three of them (Sonnets 101, 104, where 'friend' becomes 'love', and 108, where 'sweet boy' appears as 'sweet love') so that these poems appear to be addressed to a female rather than to a male. But Benson makes no consistent attempt to give the impression that the poems are addressed to a woman; other poems probably addressed to a man, including Sonnet 20, remain substantially unaltered. Interestingly, an anonymous seventeenth-century owner changed many of the titles in his copy for the better: Sonnet 20, 'The Exchange' in Benson, becomes 'The Mistress Masculine' (Rollins, ii. 22).

Benson's volume does not include the narrative poems; it reprints the whole of the already pirated *Passionate Pilgrim* from its expanded second edition of 1612; it adds many verses by writers other than Shakespeare, including Ben Jonson, Thomas Heywood, and Francis Beaumont, without identifying their authors; and it prints an appendix of 'excellent poems...by other gentlemen'. In spite of this, Benson's preface claims that all the poems are by Shakespeare, and that they had not previously been published. Astonishingly to anyone who has had to struggle with the more difficult of the sonnets, Benson in his preface claims that the poems in his volume are 'serene, clear, and elegantly plain, such gentle strains as shall recreate and not perplex your brain, no intricate or cloudy stuff to puzzle intellect, but perfect eloquence'. Some modern critics have been misled by these claims into suggesting that the poems must have seemed easier to seventeenth-century readers than they do to us, but in fact Benson did not write the preface as a response to the poems he reprints but plagiarized and paraphrased his remarks from a poem by Thomas May that has nothing to do with them or with Shakespeare.

Benson's collection might be dismissed as an aberration had it not exerted great influence for a long time. No versions of the Sonnets appeared in print during the rest of the seventeenth century, but when Charles Gildon came to prepare a supplementary volume of poems to Rowe's 1709 edition of the plays, it was Benson's book, with omissions, that formed the basis of his text. Benson was also reprinted and revised in editions of 1714, 1725, 1728, 1741, 1771, 1774, and 1775; informed a corrupt edition of 1804; and went on influencing American editions till 1818.

Although Bernard Lintott had reprinted the authentic, 1609 Quarto as part of a two-volume edition of the poems in 1711—describing it, however, as 'One hundred and Fifty Four Sonnets, all of them in Praise of his Mistress'—and George Steevens published a scholarly reprint in his *Twenty Plays of Shakespeare* in 1766, the Sonnets were read principally in Benson's mangled text until the great editor Edmond Malone edited the Quarto in his *Supplement* to the 1778 Johnson/Steevens edition of the plays in 1780. Malone's edition also formed the basis of the first American edition of the Sonnets, of 1796. He established a text that remained standard with little alteration till the Cambridge edition of 1864. Most importantly, Malone provided the first substantial scholarly, explanatory, and critical commentary, bringing his deep knowledge of the literature and manners of Shakespeare's time to bear fruitfully on the poems. Steevens had commented on Sonnet 20, 'It is impossible to read this fulsome panegyrick, addressed to a male object, without an equal mixture of disgust and indignation.' Malone, in the note in his edition of 1790, responded with an appeal to historicism: 'Some part of this indignation might perhaps have been abated, if it had been considered that such addresses to men, however indelicate, were customary in our authour's time, and neither imported criminality, nor were esteemed indecorous.... To regulate our judgment of Shakspeare's poems by the modes of modern times, is surely as unreasonable as to try his plays by the rules of Aristotle.' This argument may well be valid, and is moderately expressed, but has sometimes been regarded in modern times as an attempt to evade the homoerotic implications of the poems.

There can be no doubt that Benson's misrepresentations hindered appreciation of Shakespeare's sonnets (and of 'A Lover's Complaint') until the beginning of the Romantic period. They were responsible for an almost complete absence of critical writing and creative reappropriation (see Chapters 10 and 11, below). Benson's failure to reprint the dedication to Mr W.H. postponed discussion of their biographical implications (not necessarily a bad thing). His inclusion of poems not written by Shakespeare misled, for instance, Alexander Pope into believing that Thomas Heywood's translations of Ovid, reproduced by Benson from *The Passionate Pilgrim*, might have been Shakespeare's (Rollins, ii. 353). And although the omission of the poems from the Folio must in part be held responsible for their long-continuing absence from editions of the Complete Works, the low evaluation of the Sonnets resulting from Benson's corruptions must also have played its part.

Rehabilitation of the Sonnets was hindered too by moral objections, such as those expressed by Steevens, to love poems addressed by one man to another. This aspect of their reputation is discussed in Chapter 10, below. From around 1830 reprints of the Sonnets, sometimes in selection and in anthologies, sometimes accompanied by other poems, sometimes rearranged according to one scheme or another, sometimes accompanied by explanatory and/or critical commentary, sometimes in rethought texts, sometimes polemically presented, sometimes in facsimile of either the 1609 or the 1640 printings, sometimes including 'A Lover's Complaint' but more often not, and regularly in editions of Shakespeare's Complete Works, have abounded in ever-increasing profusion. Some have been dedicated to abstruse theses, trying to show, for example, that the poems 'belong to the Hermetic [i.e. occult] class of writings...' (written 'by the author of *Remarks on Alchemy* [E. Hitchcock]', New York, 1865).

One Gerald Massey offered to name Shakespeare's 'private friends' in *The Secret Drama of Shakespeare's Sonnets, with the Characters Identified*, first printed in 1866 but issued in a privately printed 'second and enlarged edition, limited to one hundred copies, for subscribers only', of 1872. In 1897 fifty of the sonnets were 'reprinted and interpreted with their scriptural harmonies' by 'C. E[llis]' under the title of *Shakespeare and the Bible* (1897). In a volume printed in Liverpool in 1931 Alfred Dodd presented the Sonnets as *The Personal Poems of Francis Bacon (our Shakespeare), the Son of Queen Elizabeth*. And two years later Wilde's one-time friend Lord Alfred Douglas published an edition under the title of *The True History of Shakespeare's Sonnets* (1933) arranged, with one exception, in the order recommended by Samuel Butler. In his cantankerously written introduction, which has interesting comments on Wilde's *The Portrait of Mr W.H.*, Douglas supports the idea, propagated by Wilde and Butler but originating with Malone, that the Sonnets are addressed to a William Hughes. Douglas 'utterly rejects the notion that Shakespeare was a homosexualist' (p. 19).

Some of the sonnets have been bowdlerized: Francis T. Palgrave, poet, hymn writer, and anthologist, in his edition of *Songs and Sonnets of William Shakespeare* published in the Golden Treasury Series in 1879, like Benson long before him, gave every sonnet a title, some of them in Latin (so, for example, No. 107 is 'Amor Contra Mundum'—'love against the world'). Substitution of numbers by titles helped Palgrave to conceal the fact that he omitted the two most explicitly sexual sonnets, Nos. 20 (to Alfred Douglas's dismay) and 151, as well as the last two, no doubt because of their supposed allusions to venereal disease.

Palgrave's long-popular *Golden Treasury of the Best Songs and Lyrical Poems in the English Language*, published four years earlier, had included seventeen of the sonnets. Twenty-five years later Arthur Quiller-Couch printed twenty of them in his *Oxford Book of English Verse*. Only two of these came from the second part of the sequence, both of them philosophical generalizations (Nos. 129 and 146); the same is true of Helen Gardner's selection, also of twenty (fifteen of them the same as Quiller-Couch's) in her *New Oxford Book of English Verse*, of 1972. Christopher Ricks, in his *Oxford Book of English Verse* of 1999 (which, unlike its predecessors, includes excerpts from the plays), reduces the number to eleven (three from the second part), one of which (Sonnet 55) is in part emblazoned on the dust jacket. David Norbrook and Henry Woudhuysen are more adventurous in *The Penguin Book of Renaissance Verse, 1509–1659* (1993) where their selection of sixteen of the sonnets includes the sexually explicit Nos. 20 and 135 ('Whoever hath her wish, thou hast thy Will'), which also figure among the thirty-one sonnets in the *The Norton Anthology of English Literature*, 5th edn. (1986).

The popularity of the Sonnets as love poems has resulted in many decorative printings, sometimes in fine bindings, in slip-cases, on high-quality paper, and in calligraphic form, intended as collectors' items for bibliophiles or as gifts for the beloved. Oddly polemical in intent is *Some Well-known 'Sugar'd Sonnets' by William Shakespeare, re-sugared with Ornamental Borders*, designed by Edwin J. Ellis and etched by Tristram J. Ellis (1893). A dedication addressed to 'Dear Mr W.H.' apologizes for the fact that the 'etched borders' show naked female infants disporting themselves in attitudes suggested by the ten selected sonnets that their bends adorn. The reason for the choice of 'baby-ladies' rather, presumably, than 'baby-gentlemen' is that 'the taste of the day refuses to endure such violently pretty adoration, coming from one man-friend to another, as Mr W. S addressed to you'. Illustrated editions are rarer than might be supposed; they include one (in *All the Love Poems of Shakespeare* (1947), often reprinted) with mildly erotic decorations by Eric Gill which have only limited relevance to the text. More apposite are the fine woodcuts by Agnes Miller Parker in a Heritage Press, New York edition of *The Poems of Shakespeare* (1958), edited and introduced by Peter Alexander.

Perhaps the most imaginative illustrations are the engravings by Simon Brett and others in the Folio Society's handsomely printed volume *Shakespeare's Sonnets* (it includes 'A Lover's Complaint') of 1989, based oddly on Malone's text and with an introduction by Katherine Duncan-Jones. (The Folio Society's eight-volume reprint based on the Oxford Complete Works does not include the poems.) It is currently possible to buy all the sonnets printed on a single poster, and there are a number of audio versions incorporating or based on them (surveyed in Chapter 12, below.)

Many attempts have been made to rearrange the order of the Sonnets, perhaps to increase their narrative or intellectual coherence or according to theories of versification. The monumental New Variorum edition of 1944 tabulates twenty different reorderings from 1640 to 1938. Sir Denys Bray, for example, Foreign Secretary to the Government of India, in an edition of 1925, discerned patterns of rhyme links and rearranged the sequence to take account of them; since it involves separating sonnets (such as Nos. 57 and 58) in which links of subject matter are apparent, it is not too convincing. Nevertheless it has been used to support theories that the Sonnets were written by someone other than Shakespeare. The American scholar Brents Stirling attempted a different reordering by groups in the course of a study, *The Shakespeare Sonnet Order* (1968).

In recent times it has been customary to follow Thorpe's order, not necessarily out of a belief that it was determined by Shakespeare, certainly not on the grounds that it represents the order of composition, but sometimes simply because no obviously better one has ever presented itself. Nevertheless it is as well to be aware that some reordered versions may still be in circulation. The Sonnets have also appeared in translations into hundreds of different languages. For example, as many as four separate versions in Czech appeared between 1992 and 1997. One of them (by a right-wing politician, Miroslav Macek), like Benson's of 1640, implicitly censors the poems by changing the gender of the addressee of some of them from male to female. Another of the Czech translators, Martin Hilský, has an interesting discussion of the problems and rewards of translation in his article cited in Further Reading, below. The Sonnets have even been translated into modern English in, for example, A. L. Rowse's arrogantly titled *Shakespeare's Sonnets—The Problems Solved: A modern edition with prose versions, introduction and notes* (1964; rev. 1973).

Just as, during the eighteenth century and later, the Sonnets and other poems tended to be relegated to supplementary volumes of collected editions, so too more recently in one-volume collected editions they have often been printed at the back of the book as if they were somewhat redundant appendages to the main body of their author's work. This was the practice in once standard editions such as the Globe (1864), W. J. Craig's Oxford edition (1891), G. L. Kittredge's (1936), C. J. Sisson's (1951), and Peter Alexander's (1954) editions, all of which retained the Folio order for the plays. More recently the ordering of works within editions has been rethought. So Hardin Craig's edition of 1951, which developed through successive revisions into David Bevington's of 1973, 1980, and 1997, groups the works in periods of composition, placing the Sonnets among the earliest. The Riverside, of 1974 (rev. 1997), follows the Folio in adopting a generic division but orders the plays according to a conjectural chronology within it; the Sonnets and other poems, however, come at the end. The editors of the Oxford Complete Works (1986), whose overall arrangement is chronological, print the Sonnets along with 'A Lover's Complaint' according to their conjectural date of late revision (around 1602) in the attempt to make it possible to see them in relation to the rest of Shakespeare's work.

Students of the Sonnets will benefit from critical studies such as those mentioned in the Further Reading section, but are likely also to need the kind of help with details of the texts that is provided by annotated single-volume editions. The great two-volume New Variorum edition, prepared by Hyder Edward Rollins and published in 1944, is a wonderful and heroic digest of a great mass of information, much of it curious and entertaining, indispensable to scholars and well worth consulting by the general reader, but scarcely for everyday use. Subsequent older editions, notably that by W. G. Ingram and Theodore Redpath dating back to 1964, can still be useful, but during the last quarter of the twentieth century and in the early years of the twenty-first at least six ambitious recensions of the Sonnets, usually but not always including 'A Lover's Complaint', have appeared, some of them including elaborate critical and scholarly introductions, detailed explanatory commentaries, and textual apparatus. In two of them, however, the aim is primarily critical, the texts of the poems being printed as points of reference. In what follows we discuss the editions most in currency at the time of writing, in the hope that this may provide guidance to the various kinds of assistance and stimulus they offer.

In *Shakespeare's Sonnets*, edited with analytical commentary (1977), Stephen Booth provides first a relatively short preface explaining and exemplifying the aims of his idiosyncratic edition. Then comes a facsimile of the Sonnets ('A Lover's Complaint' is omitted) from the 1609 Quarto printed in parallel with an edited text in modern spelling.

Following these—with the resultant temptation to the reader to use a different text so as not to have to move backward and forwards within the same book—comes a series of immensely detailed, primarily critical notes on each sonnet, along with appendices on 'Facts and Theories about Shakespeare's Sonnets' and excerpts from Golding's translation of Ovid's *Metamorphoses*. A detailed index facilitates use of the notes as a commentary on Shakespeare's language. On Shakespeare's sexuality, Booth famously and caustically remarks 'William Shakespeare was almost certainly homosexual, bisexual, or heterosexual. The sonnets provide no evidence on the matter' (Booth, *Sonnets*, p. 548).

Booth's learned and often witty commentary is controlled by a passionately held desire 'to recommend an unmediated analysis of works of art (or an analysis that at least tries to resist mediation), an analysis that is not satisfying in anything like the way in which its subject is satisfying, an analysis that does not try to decide which of a poem's actions should be acknowledged but instead tries to explain the means by which all a poem's improbably sorted actions coexist and cohere within the poem and, for the duration of the poem, within the mind of its reader' (Booth, *Sonnets*, p. 515).

The complexity and length of Booth's exegesis derive largely from his concern to trace the process of readerly apprehension moment by moment, so that meanings are in a constant state of flux: 'a word or phrase can be incomprehensible at the moment it is read and then be effectively glossed by the lines that follow it; a word or phrase can (and in the sonnets regularly does) have one meaning as a reader comes on it, another as its sentence concludes, and a third when considered from the vantage point of a summary statement in the couplet' (Booth, *Sonnets*, p. x). This critical technique does not make for easy reading, and is very much geared to the conscious and subconscious mind processes of a modern reader, but has the valuable effect of opening up the poems rather than closing them down, as conventional explanations are liable to do. Never before had the Sonnets been subjected to a scrutiny so rigorous, scholarly, and sensitive to the intellectual and associative effects of language.

Another, no less idiosyncratic, edition that is primarily critical in intent is Helen Vendler's more recent *The Art of Shakespeare's Sonnets* (1997). The book is an edition rather than a critical study only in the sense that, like Booth's, it reprints all the sonnets (again omitting 'A Lover's Complaint'), both in facsimile and in a modernized text, and that it provides an independent commentary written in the form of an essay after each of them. Vendler's introduction explaining her critical approach is a dense, wonderfully rich essay which places great emphasis on the poems' dynamic, the relationship between poet and speaker, the shifts of tone and voice within a single sonnet. Convinced that 'A writer of Shakespeare's seriousness writes from internal necessity', and asking 'What is the inner agenda of the *Sonnets*? What are their compositional motivations? What does a writer gain from working, over and over, in one subgenre?', she finds that Shakespeare 'learned to find strategies to enact feeling in form, feelings in forms, multiplying both to a superlative degree through 154 poems. No poet has ever found more linguistic forms by which to replicate human responses than Shakespeare in the *Sonnets*' (Vendler, p. 17). It is significant that, like Samuel Butler before her, Vendler 'found it necessary to learn the *Sonnets* by heart' (p. 11); significant too that in her first edition she included her own (rather disappointing) recording of a selection of the poems because she found that actors 'speak the lines with constant mis-emphases, destroying the meaning of many of the sonnets by not observing inner antitheses and parallels' (p. 37). In her teacherly expositions of individual sonnets she writes brilliantly about each poem in the sequence, seeking to draw out its verbal patterns, making much of its structural features, the relationship of one quatrain to another, of the octave to the sestet, of the couplet to the whole, of what she calls 'couplet ties'—words whose repetition links the couplet to the rest of the poem. She draws attention, too, to the relationship of each poem to others in the sequence. From time to time she resorts to diagrams to clarify relationships and to demonstrate patterns while conceding that 'irritated readers can skip my schemes and simply read the Commentary without them' (p. xvii). She proceeds on the assumption that the poems are printed in an order determined by Shakespeare and, like most editors, that all the poems up to No. 126 are addressed not only to a young man, but to the same young man, a position that we question.

Vendler's are not easy readings of the Sonnets; and her book—like the Sonnets themselves—is, as she admits, not easy to read from beginning to end, but readers feeling that they have exhausted a particular sonnet could not fail to find fresh stimulus and illumination from her commentaries.

More conventional—though no less valuable—editions are available in all the major series. John Kerrigan's New Penguin of 1986 not merely includes 'A Lover's Complaint' but argues strongly for the cumulative effect both of the Sonnets in relation to each other and of 'A Lover's Complaint' in relation to them. Contemporary readers, he is convinced, 'would have read the volume *as* a volume, and their sense of the parts would have been modified by the whole' (Kerrigan, p. 14). In his long and critically acute introduction Kerrigan writes persuasively of 'that subtle modulation of material from poem to poem into the form of the whole which makes reading Shakespeare's Sonnets such a concentrated yet essentially cumulative experience' (p. 8). The continuities convince Kerrigan that the poems, not written in the order in which they are printed, nevertheless need no reordering. If they are not directly autobiographical, there are 'so many points in the sequence at which obscurity appears to stem not from failing verbal powers but from an unwillingness to grapple painful emotions into form that it seems reasonable to infer a troubled author behind the poetic "I"' (p. 11). Kerrigan stresses the 'deep disapproval which homosexual activity attracted in Elizabethan England' (p. 46), but finds close affinities between Shakespeare, Marlowe, and Barnfield in their attitudes to homoerotic friendship: 'In the last analysis, what one finds registered in the Sonnets is profound homosexual attachment of a scarcely sensual, almost unrealized kind.' But the sonnets 'to the dark lady extend and degrade the rival attractions of heterosexual passion' (p. 55).

The New Cambridge (1997), edited by G. Blakemore Evans, lacks unity in that the introduction is written not by the editor but by a poet and critic, Anthony Hecht. This critical essay concentrates on close readings of several of the poems while also offering basic information on publication, conventions of the genre, and metrics. It pays no real attention, however, to other modern criticism. The poems are printed two to a page, with textual collations at the foot; as a result the commentary notes are separated from the poems to which they refer. Evans's concise but informative 'Introductory Note to the Commentary' repeats some of the facts given by Hecht. He asks the right basic questions, admitting that not all the first 126 poems are certainly addressed to 'a young man, or even to the same young man' (p. 112). The commentary offers scholarly and detailed but businesslike notes drawing on an exceptionally wide range of reading, and there is an excellent textual analysis.

Like Kerrigan, Katherine Duncan-Jones, in her Arden edition (1997), emphasizes the integrity of the 1609 volume. More than any other editor she insists on the Shakespearian authority of the Quarto. *Shakespeare's Sonnets*, she claims, is the author's title, not just a publisher's description of its contents. 'A Lover's Complaint' 'is not merely a formal pendant to the sonnets, but a carefully balanced thematic counterpart to them' (Duncan-Jones, p. 92). Her questionable contention that the 1609 Quarto 'reflects the minutiae, as well as the substance, of a copy manuscript certainly authorized, and perhaps also penned, by Shakespeare himself' (p. xiv) relates to her belief that 'the whole sequence as published in 1609 was put into its final shape after 1603, and possibly quite close to its printing' (p. xv). Her lengthy and lively introduction concerns itself, in so far as the distinction is valid, rather with scholarly and historical than with critical matters. Ready to believe that the poems reflect Shakespeare's personal experience, and that only one 'young man' is involved, she adopts a largely biographical approach, coming out in favour of William Herbert (to whom she devotes the better part of seventeen pages) as the male addressee. She is more receptive to the Sonnets' homoerotic implications than any previous editor, claiming of her edition that 'their homoeroticism is here confronted positively, and is newly contextualized within the powerfully "homosocial" world of James i's court' (p. xv). In keeping with this, she makes interesting use of attitudes to sexuality, especially to the Oscar Wilde case, in discussing the poems' reception. She exaggerates what she calls the 'outrageous misogyny' (p. 50) of the 'Dark Lady' Sonnets, describing the woman, in spite of the declarations of love in, for example, Nos. 127, 128, 130, 132, 139, and 141, as 'no more than a sexual convenience' (p. 51), and (encouraged perhaps by her wish to see the collection as a unified sequence) is credulous of numerological interpretations, suggesting with dubious logic that the procreation sonnets are seventeen in number because 'eighteen was the age at which young men were believed to be ready for consummated marriage' (p. 99), and seeing significance in the idea that 'the total of these "dark lady" sonnets is twenty-eight, corresponding with the lunar month or menstrual cycle' (p. 49). Her notes, frank in explications of sexuality and, like her introduction, exceptionally well informed in the literature of the period, are helpfully printed on the pages facing the poems.

Whereas all the editions so far surveyed separate the Sonnets from Shakespeare's other poems, Colin Burrow adopts a holistic approach in his Oxford edition of the *Complete Sonnets and Poems* (2002). Endorsing the view that the Sonnets are very likely printed in an order 'at least provisionally determined by Shakespeare', he admits uncertainty about their dates of composition, their biographical relevance, and the significance of the dedication, but does not dismiss these topics as irrelevant. 'The Sonnets', he writes, 'are best viewed not as Shakespeare's final triumphant assertion of poetic mastery, but as poems which develop the methods of the earlier narrative poems to their utmost point—a point at which one is not quite sure who is male and who is female, who is addressed or why, or what their respective social roles are' (Burrow, p. 91). Like many scholars before him, he counters the common view that the dedication refers to Pembroke on the grounds that it is 'extremely unlikely that an Earl should be addressed by a printer as "Mr". For a printed poem by a commoner to address an Earl as the "master mistress of my passion" (20, l. 2) would be audacious beyond belief' (Burrow, p. 100). He accepts the stylometric work of MacDonald P. Jackson (see pp. 37–8, above), while admitting 'many grey areas'. Burrow writes with particular subtlety about the difficulty of reading the collection as a 'sequence': 'the sequence calls for a form of disappointed wonder, as readers make and remake different methods of unifying the sequence' (p. 110). At the same time, however, he is sensitive to interrelationships from one poem to another and to the cumulative complexity of the collection: these are 'poems in which praise and dispraise restlessly mingle and fuse, and in which love and praise and obeisance will not be separated cleanly from hurt, and a desire to hurt back' (p. 138). He tends to write of the first 126 sonnets as poems written to one particular male friend while admitting that this is not necessarily so and indeed that many of them 'carefully skirt around even giving a fixed gender to their addressee' (p. 123). Burrow insists on ambivalence of readerly response: 'So should readers of the Sonnets give up on the real pleasure and the real and liberating disturbance which comes from thinking that

Shakespeare was homosexual? Yes and no.... The closer the poems come to a carnal revelation, the more involved their resistance to final exposure becomes, and the more insistently their words resist the imposition of a single sense upon them' (pp. 130–1). The mistress, too, is 'a complicated poetic creation, and like the "friend" is a different sort of thing in different poems' (p. 131). Concluding that 'the poems are not confessional, and . . . do not give us any insights into the heart of Shakespeare, or what he did in the bedroom', he nevertheless sees them 'in their continual counterpointing of language against implied circumstance' as 'the culmination of Shakespeare's career as a poet' (p. 138). Burrow's helpful annotation, empirical rather than, like Booth's, associative in its methods, sexually frank and acutely sensitive to linguistic nuance, continues and deepens the critical investigations of his introduction.

It is symptomatic of the Sonnets' complex, elusive, and enigmatic nature that they respond as well as they do to so wide a variety of editorial treatment and to a multitude of critical approaches.

The Critical Reputation of the Sonnets

It may be salutary to consider how the reputation of both individual sonnets and the collection as a whole has fluctuated over the centuries. Such an exercise may be revealing, too, about the topics of discussion that the poems may provoke. In this chapter we aim to provide a brief overview of the reputation of the Sonnets from the seventeenth to the twentieth century.

We have referred in Chapter 9 to the neglect of the Sonnets stemming from their omission from the First Folio and its successors, and to the fact that no texts with any real claim to authenticity, in being edited from the Quarto of 1609, were readily available until the publication of Malone's edition of 1780. Although the narrative poems remained popular in successive reprints through most of the seventeenth century, there is a total gap in printings of the Sonnets between 1640 and 1709. So it is not surprising that *The Shakspere Allusion Book* records virtually no reference to the Sonnets between 1640 and 1700—the date at which its survey concludes—and that only a few additions to its record have been made in the many years since that compilation appeared. But an interesting later discovery is a manuscript note of around 1613 in which Shakespeare's friend Leonard Digges, author of memorial verses in the First Folio, says—very much as a compliment—that sonnets by Lope de Vega are regarded in Spain 'as in England we should of our Will. Shakespeare'.[1] And there is one seventeenth-century poet and dramatist, Sir John Suckling—a great admirer and plagiarist of Shakespeare who had himself painted by

Van Dyck holding a copy of either the First or Second Folio open at *Hamlet*—who clearly knew the Sonnets well. He draws on six of them in his tragedy *Brennoralt*, published in 1640. Most of his borrowings are spoken by a woman, Iphigene, disguised as a man: for instance, her dying words, spoken to the man she loves, are

> For I like testy sick men at their death
> Would know no news but health from the physician—

a clear echo of Sonnet 140:

> As testy sick men, when their deaths be near,
> No news but health from their physicians know.
>
> (ll. 7–8)

It is easy for us to forget that during the seventeenth and eighteenth centuries old books were not easy of access, even to many scholars. Nicholas Rowe, editor of the first Collected Works, of 1709, did not know the 1609 Quarto of the Sonnets and came upon Benson's volume only when he had almost completed his task, remarking that 'There is a book of poems published in 1640 under the name of Mr William Shakespeare, but as I have but very lately seen it, without an opportunity of making any judgement upon it, I won't pretend to determine whether it be his or no' (cited in Rollins, ii. 33). And later in the century, in 1767, the great editor Edward Capell noted the existence of the 1609 Quarto while remarking that he had never seen a copy; he knew Lintott's 1711 reprint, however, and praised the Sonnets in that 'a single thought, vary'd and put in language poetical, is the subject of each sonnet; a thing essential to these compositions and yet but rarely observ'd by either ancient or modern dealers in them' (cited in Rollins, ii. 335).

An early critical comment comes from Charles Gildon, who in 1710 and 1714 published the poems as a supplement to Rowe's edition, and who remarked of the Sonnets (which he calls epigrams) that 'there is a wonderful smoothness in many of them that makes the blood dance to its numbers' (cited in Rollins, ii. 333). He was, however, fooled by Benson into mistaking some of Heywood's poems for Shakespeare's. It is notable that none of the great names in Shakespeare criticism before the Romantic period—John Dryden, Alexander Pope, Dr Johnson—offers any critical comment on the Sonnets.

George Steevens, who failed to remedy the omission of all the non-dramatic verse in his 1778 revision of Johnson's edition, contributed to Malone's of 1780 a number of notes expressing extreme distaste for the sonnet form. Malone himself was not strong in defence of Shakespeare's use of it, finding 'a want of variety' while admitting that the versification 'is smooth and harmonious' and that some of the sonnets 'are written with perspicuity and energy' (cited in Rollins, ii. 337). Steevens, who for decades was seen as the villain of sonnet criticism, was far more extreme in his much-quoted condemnation of the Sonnets, along with the other poems, in his 1793 edition: 'We have not reprinted the Sonnets etc. of Shakespeare because the strongest act of parliament that could be framed would fail to compel readers into their service'; moral objections are suggested by his reference to the 'implements of criticism' of 'their only intelligent editor, Malone' as being 'like the ivory rake and golden spade in Prudentius, which are on this occasion disgraced by the objects of their culture' (cited in Rollins, ii. 337–8). The allusion (rarely explained) is to a poem in which the Latin poet castigates an orator, Symmachus, for misusing his talents by propagating paganism, comparing this to the use of precious tools for muck-raking. By analogy, Steevens implies that Shakespeare is abusing his talents in celebrating a homoerotic relationship. He thus appears to be the first writer to voice more or less explicit objections to the poems on moral as well as aesthetic grounds.

The very form of the sonnet was unfashionable during the eighteenth century and later. Johnson, in his *Dictionary* of 1755, says that it is 'not very suitable to the English language, and has not been used by any man of eminence since Milton'; he glosses the word 'sonneteer' as 'a small poet, [said] in contempt' (cited in Rollins, ii. 338–9). Later, in 1813, Byron was to write in a letter that 'I never wrote but one sonnet before . . . and I will never write another. They are the most puling, petrifying stupidly platonic compositions' (cited in Rollins, ii. 341).

Nevertheless, interest in Shakespeare's use of the form had increased with the Romantics, though comment tends to take the shape only of generalized value judgements, often unfavourable, mixed at times with doubts about the propriety of addressing love poems to a man. Wordsworth, the first major English poet to take up the sonnet form since Milton, writing in a manuscript note (now in the Folger Shakespeare Library) some time before 1803, found the

'Dark Lady' Sonnets 'worse than a puzzle-peg. They are abominably harsh, obscure, and worthless' (a similar view was to be expressed far later by several American poets—see below). 'The others are for the most part much better, have many fine lines very fine lines and passages. They are also in many places warm with passion.' ('Warm' at this time was coming to mean, as the *Oxford English Dictionary* puts it, 'indelicate in its appeal to sexual emotion'.) Wordsworth concludes, 'Their chief faults—and heavy ones they are—are sameness, tediousness, quaintness, and elaborate obscurity' (cited in Rollins, ii. 347).

The Sonnets' 'warmth' was to be noted by other contemporary writers but did not always inhibit admiration. William Hazlitt, in the *Characters of Shakespear's Plays* of 1817, wrote, 'The subject of them seems to be somewhat equivocal' (presumably alluding to many of them being addressed to a male), 'but many of them are highly beautiful in themselves, and interesting as they relate to the state of the personal feelings of the author' (cited in Rollins, ii. 350). And in 1803, Coleridge, recommending his 7-year-old son Hartley to read the Sonnets, nevertheless finds it necessary to write (admittedly at half past three on a November morning in the Lake District) 'O my son! I pray fervently that thou may'st know inwardly how impossible it was for a Shakespeare not to have been in his heart's heart chaste' (cited in Rollins, ii. 347–8). This belief no doubt contributed to Coleridge's astonishing view, expressed in his *Table Talk* (14 May 1833), that 'the sonnets could only have come from a man deeply in love, and in love with a woman; and there is one sonnet which, from its incongruity, I take to be a purposed blind'. (Presumably, though oddly, he is thinking of Sonnet 20.)

Although in *Biographia Literaria* (1817) Coleridge wrote brilliantly and enthusiastically about the narrative poems, he fluctuated in his opinion of the Sonnets: 'Shakespeare', he said while lecturing on Donne, 'is never *positively* bad, even in his Sonnets', though later he was to say that they are characterized 'by boundless fertility and laboured condensation of thought, with perfection of sweetness in rhythm and metre' (cited in Rollins, ii. 349).

Perhaps the first passionately wholehearted admirer of the Sonnets is John Keats, who, in 'On Sitting Down to read *King Lear* Again' (1818), was to write one of the finest poetic responses to Shakespeare, itself in sonnet form. Even Keats, however, seems to have admired the

Sonnets mainly for incidental felicities. In a letter of 22 November 1817 he wrote in a letter to his friend John Hamilton Reynolds

> I ne'er found so many beauties in the Sonnets—they seem to be full of fine things said unintentionally—in the intensity of working out conceits. Is this to be borne? Hark ye!
>
> > When lofty trees I see barren of praise
> > > Which erst from heat did canopy the herd,
> > And summer's green all girded up with sheaves,
> > > Borne on the bier with white and bristly beard.
>
> He has left nothing to say about nothing or anything...He overwhelms a genuine lover of poesy with all manner of abuse talking about
>
> > > a poet's rage,
> > > And stretched meter of an antique song.[2]

But a couple of years later Keats, in search of 'a better Sonnet Stanza than we have', complained that a Shakespearian sonnet 'appears too elegiac—and the couplet at the end of it has seldom a pleasing effect'.[3] Nevertheless one of Keats's best sonnets, 'When I have fears that I may cease to be', is strongly Shakespearian in form—indeed, Jonathan Bate describes it as 'an imitation or highly accomplished pastiche of a Shakespearean sonnet'.[4] 'Only with Keats', Bate writes, 'did Shakespeare's sonnets have a profound effect on the poetic practice of an English Romantic.'[5]

Later in his life Wordsworth was to defend the form of the sonnet against its detractors and to make what has become one of the best-known of all comments on Shakespeare's use of it in a poem which itself is in sonnet form and which offers a whistle-stop survey of its use by other poets, both British and international:

> Scorn not the Sonnet; Critic, you have frowned,
> Mindless of its just honours; with this key
> Shakespeare unlocked his heart; the melody
> Of this small lute gave ease to Petrarch's wound;
> A thousand times this pipe did Tasso sound;
> Camoëns soothed with it an exile's grief;
> The Sonnet glittered a gay myrtle leaf
> Amid the cypress with which Dante crowned
> His visionary brow: a glow-worm lamp,
> It cheered mild Spenser, called from Faeryland

> To struggle through dark ways; and, when a damp
> Fell round the path of Milton, in his hand
> The Thing became a trumpet, whence he blew
> Soul-animating strains—alas, too few!
>
> ('Scorn not the Sonnet', 1827)

The words 'with this key | Shakespeare unlocked his heart' encapsulate a point of view that has been vigorously contested in innumerable contributions to a debate that will never be resolved. Do these poems really give us access to Shakespeare's inmost feelings, or are they exercises of technical virtuosity—or, perhaps, some one, some the other, some more, others less so?

There was certainly a growing interest in the biographical implications of the poems. Perhaps the first book entirely devoted to the subject is James Boaden's *On the Sonnets of Shakespeare* (1837), which put forward William Herbert, Earl of Pembroke as the youth, and was rapidly followed by *Shakespeare's Autobiographical Poems: Being his Sonnets Clearly Developed with His Character chiefly drawn from his Work* (1838) by Keats's friend Charles Armitage Brown. As its epigraph this book has what is virtually a self-quotation from one of its later chapters, and is clearly influenced by Wordsworth: 'With this key, simple as it may appear, every difficulty is unlocked, and we have nothing but pure uninterrupted biography.' The 'key' is the revelation vouchsafed to Brown that the Quarto volume actually consists not of 154 poems but of six, each made up of a group of stanzas in sonnet form. Brown's projected edition of the sonnets themselves, advertised at the end of his study as 'Preparing for the Press', seems not to have materialized.

As the century draws on, more appreciative, even effusive comments are to be found; so Edward Fitzgerald (1809–83), translator of *The Rubáiyát of Omar Khayyám*, friend of Tennyson, lover of boys and men, wrote in 1832 that he 'had but half an idea of him [Shakespeare], Demigod as he seemed before, till I read [the Sonnets] carefully' (letter of 27 November 1832, cited in Rollins, ii. 356). Unfortunately he did not expatiate on what he found in them. In the same year the scholar Alexander Dyce castigated Steevens for his contempt, writing that the Sonnets 'contain such a quantity of profound thought as must astonish every reflecting reader; they are adorned by splendid and delicate imagery; they are sublime, pathetic, tender, or sweetly playful; while they delight the ear by their fluency, and their varied harmonies of rhythm' (cited in Rollins, ii. 356). It is during the 1830s too that editions of the Sonnets begin to multiply; Rollins (ii. 361) writes that 'after 1830 scarcely a year passed without at least one edition's being published'. Yet in 1838 the poet Thomas Campbell, in his edition of Shakespeare's *Works* (1842 edn., p. xxvi), wrote that 'As a whole, however, these sonnets are no more to our poet's fame, than a snowball on the top of Olympus.'

Twenty years after Wordsworth's came another well-known sonnet directly inspired by Shakespeare, though not referring to his practice as a sonneteer, by Matthew Arnold:

> Others abide our question. Thou art free.
> We ask and ask: Thou smilest and art still,
> Out-topping knowledge. For the loftiest hill,
> That to the stars uncrowns his majesty,
> Planting his steadfast footsteps in the sea,
> Making the Heaven of Heavens his dwelling-place,
> Spares but the cloudy border of his base
> To the foil'd searching of mortality:
> And thou, who didst the stars and sunbeams know,
> Self-school'd, self-scann'd, self-honour'd, self-secure,
> Didst walk on earth unguess'd at. Better so!
> All pains the immortal spirit must endure,
>   All weakness that impairs, all griefs that bow,
>   Find their sole voice in that victorious brow.
>
> ('Shakespeare', 1849)

It is of course far from true that Shakespeare was 'Self-school'd', 'self-honour'd', or that he walked 'on earth unguessed at'. The idea that he 'Out-top[s] knowledge' appears to deny the possibility of seeing into his heart even in the most apparently intimate of his poems. And this attitude foreshadows the aggressive reply to Wordsworth from Robert Browning, himself a practitioner of a form of poetic fiction—the dramatic soliloquy—which may be likened to the pseudo-confessional sonnet. In his poem 'House' of 1876 Browning cites Wordsworth only to refute him:

> Hoity-toity! A street to explore,
>   Your house the exception! '*With this same key*
> *Shakespeare unlocked his heart*', once more!
>   Did Shakespeare? If so, the less Shakespeare he!

But the Sonnets remained fascinating to readers seeking revelations of Shakespeare's personality and of his artistic achievement, if not of his day-to-day life. Francis T. Palgrave was to write in 1865 that 'there is, after all, nothing more remarkable or fascinating in English poetry than these personal revelations of the mind of our greatest poet. We read them again and again, and find each time some new proof of his almost superhuman insight into human nature; of his unrivalled mastery over all the tones of love' (*Songs and Sonnets of William Shakespeare* (1879 edn.), 243).

Negative views continued to be expressed. Henry Hallam (father of Tennyson's friend Arthur), in his *Introduction to the Literature of Europe* (1839, iii. 289–91), continued the line of criticism represented by Steevens, saying (with a plethora of negatives) that he found it 'impossible not to wish that Shakespeare had never written them. There is a weakness and folly in all excessive and misplaced affection, which is not redeemed by the touches of nobler sentiments that abound in this long series of sonnets' (cited in Rollins, ii. 359). Tennyson himself, however, was to counter this around 1883 with 'Henry Hallam made a great mistake about them; they are noble' (cited in Rollins, ii. 364). But Benjamin Jowett, the translator of Plato and Master of Balliol College, Oxford, disapproved of Tennyson's enthusiasm, and in doing so expressed his own sense that they are homoerotic—and, by covert implication, that the same was true of Tennyson's love for the dead Arthur Hallam: 'He would have seemed to me to be reverting for a moment to the great sorrow of his own mind. . . . The love of the sonnets which he so strikingly expressed was a sort of sympathy with Hellenism' (cited in Duncan-Jones, p. 79; see Chapter 11, below, for a discussion of Tennyson's *In Memoriam*). Towards the close of the century, in 1899, Samuel Butler (who was bisexual) also invokes the Greeks; writing more sympathetically, if circumspectly and disingenuously, he compares Shakespeare to Homer (whose works, he had argued at book-length, were written by a woman), remarking that

Fresh from the study of the other great work in which the love that passeth the love of women is portrayed as nowhere else save in the Sonnets, I cannot but be struck with the fact that it is in the two greatest of all poets that we find this subject treated with the greatest intensity of feeling. The marvel, however, is this; that whereas the love of Achilles for Patroclus depicted by the Greek poet is purely English, absolutely without taint or alloy of any kind, the love of the English poet for Mr W.H. was, though only for a short time, more Greek than English.[6]

Butler thought Shakespeare had a brief but consummated encounter with a sailor boy (see Chapter 3, above), but veils his views in timorous obscurity.

Moral disapproval was at times vehement. A German scholar who wrote extensively about the Sonnets, Hermann Conrad (whose surname was originally Isaac, suggesting that perhaps he had experience in concealing truths that he preferred not to acknowledge), wrote in

Fig. 11. Simon Brett's witty engraving superimposing an image of Shakespeare's face on a representation of Oscar Wilde illustrates the Folio Society edition (1989) of the Sonnets.

1879 of a 'moral duty' to show that the Sonnets reveal none of the 'loathsome, sensual degeneracy of love among friends that antiquity unfortunately knew'. The answer, according to Conrad, lay in Platonism (cited in Rollins, ii. 233). The Swedish dramatist August Strindberg (1849–1912) wrote the word 'Shit!!!' on the title-page of a Swedish translation, but this unsubtle form of criticism tells us nothing of the exact grounds of his dislike.[7]

Moral criticism of the Sonnets was exacerbated in many people's eyes by Oscar Wilde's interest in them, evinced at greatest length in his short story *The Portrait of Mr W.H.*, first published in 1889 (an expanded version was lost and did not appear until 1921), which demonstrates a remarkably close knowledge of the poems and of scholarship surrounding them. In this 'minor triumph of literary art, homo-erotic fantasy successfully masquerades as fiction and criticism, the whole sufficiently sublimated so as not to disturb the staid sensibilities of readers of *Blackwood's Magazine*', writes S. Schoenbaum.[8] At his trial in 1895 Wilde responded eloquently to a request to explain the words 'The love that dare not speak its name', from a poem by his lover Lord Alfred Douglas called 'Two Loves', with:

'The Love that dare not speak its name' in this century is such a great affection of an elder for a younger man as there was between David and Jonathan, such as Plato made the very basis of his philosophy, and such as you find in the sonnets of Michelangelo and Shakespeare. It is that deep, spiritual affection that is as pure as it is perfect. It dictates and pervades great works of art like those of Shakespeare and Michelangelo, and those two letters of mine, such as they are. It is in this century misunderstood, so much misunderstood that it may be described as the 'Love that dare not speak its name,' and on account of it I am placed where I am now. It is beautiful, it is fine, it is the noblest form of affection. There is nothing unnatural about it. It is intellectual, and it repeatedly exists between an elder and a younger man, when the elder man has intellect, and the younger man has all the joy, hope and glamour of life before him. That it should be so the world does not understand. The world mocks at it and sometimes puts one in the pillory for it.[9]

But for most people Wilde was an unsuccessful advocate. In 1905 Sidney Lee, introducing an Oxford facsimile of the Quarto, declared that 'a purely literal interpretation of the impassioned protestations of affection for a "lovely boy" which course through the sonnets, ... casts a slur on the dignity of the poet's name which scarcely bears discussion'. These poems fail to express that 'friendship of the healthy manly type' (p. 11) of which the plays give many instances. Lee found his escape route in the notion that they are written within a convention of flattery to a patron.

It is remarkable that at least up to the end of the nineteenth century women readers had little to say about the Sonnets. The compilers of the anthology *Women Reading Shakespeare 1660–1900* (1997), Ann Thompson and Sasha Roberts, include little on the Sonnets and poems 'simply because women do not seem to have written about them very much'.[10] Not until the very end of their period do they find anything worth reprinting; this is a passage by one Laura Rossi, published in 1897 in a book, *Side-Lights on Shakespeare*, designed 'to supply the information required by students preparing for examinations' as well as to appeal 'to the general reader', and written in collaboration with Elvina Mary Corbould. Like many writers of her period, Rossi finds the poems interesting mainly for the light they throw on their author's personality:

It is certain that through the sonnets we may approach more nearly to the man Shakespeare than by any of the plays. He lays bare the deepest feelings of his passionate heart, and shows a side of his character unrevealed to any friend. Who could have supposed that the man who carved his way from rustic obscurity to triumphant success had in him such a capacity for a feminine depth of devotion? or that a man who had so keen an interest in property could plead so piteously for love?[11]

Equating the poetic 'I' with Shakespeare's autobiographical self means that Rossi and Corbould remain closed to the possibility of imagining a female persona as the poetic voice.

Around the turn of the century much interest is displayed in the Sonnets as direct autobiography, and especially in the identity of the 'dark lady'. An eccentric named Thomas Tyler was an obsessive and, for a while, influential advocate of Mary Fitton, one of Queen Elizabeth's maids of honour who was the mistress of Pembroke, who thus by implication is identified as the young man. Tyler's theory, propounded in his edition of 1890, attracted distinguished supporters including such scholars as F. J. Furnivall, Georg Brandes, and Sidney Lee, but collapsed when two portraits of Mary Fitton turned up, showing beyond dispute that she was fair of complexion, grey-eyed, and brown-haired. This was in 1897, but the theory was not easily scotched. The colourful charlatan Frank Harris revived it first in his play *Shakespeare and his Love* (1904)—wisely rejected for performance by Herbert Beerbohm Tree—and again in his pseudo-biography *The Man Shakespeare and his Tragic Life-Story* (1909), which finds self-portraits everywhere in Shakespeare's writings and was hailed by many readers as a revelation. Fitton also figures as Shakespeare's mistress in Harris's sequel, *The Women of Shakespeare* (1911), in which he identifies her with Helen in *All's Well That Ends Well*, and the Earl of Pembroke with Bertram in the same play.

In the meantime Bernard Shaw had written his brief skit *The Dark Lady of the Sonnets* (1909), essentially a piece of propaganda on behalf of a national theatre, in which Harley Granville-Barker played Shakespeare when it was performed at the Haymarket Theatre in London. This too shows Fitton as the dark lady, though in his extended preface, which includes a wonderful pen portrait of Tyler, Shaw says he knows she wasn't, and that 'she might have been Maria Tompkins for all I cared'.[12] He also says he prefers the more recent theory that she was Mrs Davenant. Another dramatist, Clemence Dane (pseudonym of Winifred Ashton, 1888–1965), was also not deterred by the evidence against Fitton, portraying her in her prepos-terous but once popular play *William Shakespeare* of 1921 as first Shakespeare's, then Marlowe's mistress; Shakespeare, still in love with her after Marlowe has seduced her, accidentally kills him at Deptford in an episode resembling the real-life death of Marlowe as well as the fictional death of Mercutio, in *Romeo and Juliet*.

Not all writers approved the quarrying of the Sonnets for infor-mation about their author's life. In 1911 John Masefield deplored what he saw as the fact that interest in the Sonnets as autobiography was supplanting appreciation of Shakespeare's true genius: 'That they are now widely read while the plays are seldom acted, is another proof that this age cares more for what was perishing and personal in Shakespeare than for that which went winging on, in the great light, surveying the eternal nature of man.'[13] Masefield might have been even more scornful if he had known to what extent the Sonnets would become a hunting ground for anti-Stratfordians, as is still true—*The Story the Sonnets Tell* (1995) is the title of a long study by A. D. Wraight attempting to prove that Shakespeare is the pseudonym of a resurrected Christopher Marlowe—but this is a plot we shall not till here.

Masefield's dismissal of biographical interpretation had been fore-shadowed in George Wyndham's edition of 1898 in which, Hallett Smith was to write in his book *The Tension of the Lyre* (1981), for the first time 'someone is reading the sonnets as poetry'.[14] But, as we have seen in Chapter 3, nothing can stem the flood of attempts to identify both a male and a female recipient of sonnets by Shakespeare. And opinions about the poems' moral stance continue to be expressed. In *On Reading Shakespeare* (1931), the American essayist Logan Pearsall Smith wrote ironically that

The story Shakespeare recounts of his moral—or rather his immoral—pre-dicament between these 'two loves' of his—*Two loves I have of comfort and despair*—must certainly, in the interests of the British Empire, be smothered up; the business of proving and re-proving, and proving over again—and then proving still once more, just to be absolutely certain—that our Shakespeare cannot possibly mean what he so frankly tells us, has become almost a national industry.[15]

A number of poet-critics, especially in America, were far from whole-hearted in their admiration of the poems. John Crowe Ransom, in an essay of 1937–8, found Shakespeare a careless workman, and the poems generally ill-constructed, with the logical pattern failing to match the metrical pattern. It is not always easy to be sure whether criticism based apparently on aesthetic criteria is nevertheless influenced by moral judgement. Yvor Winters, lecturing to undergraduates in 1963, said he wished Shakespeare had thrown the manuscript of his 'embar-rassing sonnets' into the fire.[16] And John Berryman, who deplored 'the humiliating privacy of some of their subject matter', shared Words-worth's view that the last group 'are mostly very bad poetry indeed, contemptuous, trivial, and obscene'.[17] W. H. Auden, in his introduc-tion to the Signet edition (1964), remarked, reasonably enough, on the Sonnets' uneven merit as poems. He explains: 'On going through the hundred and fifty-four of the Sonnets, I find forty-nine which seem to me excellent throughout, a good number of the rest have one or two memorable lines, but there are also several which I can only read out of a sense of duty' (p. xxiv). Unfortunately Auden does not identify which sonnets constitute his preferences. In 1977 the British poet Gavin Ewart (1916–95), best known as the author of the much-anthologized lines beginning 'Miss Twy was soaping her breasts in the bath', wrote, in a somewhat irregular sonnet titled 'Shakespeare's Universality',

> It's interesting that Shakespeare's Sonnets, which are
> (I think we can't doubt) completely based on his life,
> are by a long way his least satisfactory verse.
> It's better for a writer, in most cases, to get out and about.
> If he gets stuck in his own psyche for too long
> he bores everybody—and that includes himself.[18]

It seems fair to say that during the later part of the twentieth century the Sonnets' reputation was enhanced by two principal factors. Relaxation of moral disapproval based on the possible homoeroticism of many poems in the collection followed the decriminalization of homosexual acts between consenting adults in Great Britain in 1967. The other, deriving in part from the tidal wave of academic criticism that has its beginnings in the second and third decades of the century, is a broader responsiveness to the fluctuations of poetic style to be found in the collection, so that for example the more metaphysical poems, including some of those in the later part, are no less valued than the more lyrical ones favoured by earlier generations. But it is probably also true to say that the popularity of the collection is not commensurate with the number of copies in circulation; the reputation of the Sonnets as the greatest of all collections of love poetry is based on relatively few of the individual poems, and owners are more likely to read in the collection than to read through it. What Lord Alfred Douglas wrote in 1933 may be true today: 'very few, even among the most cultivated, really read the Sonnets (except perhaps about a dozen of the best known)' (*True History of Shakespeare's Sonnets* (1933), p. vi).

The Sonnets and Later Writers

In his twenty-one-lined 'American Sonnet' (1991), Billy Collins describes the effect of a sonnet as

> a few square inches of where we have strayed
> And a compression of what we feel.[1]

Writers of poetry, prose, and drama have long drawn inspiration from Shakespeare's sonnets, reappropriating their ideas and language to create new meanings, to compress, explore, and evolve other thoughts and emotions. What follows is a selective survey of the many writings which represent an ongoing effect of cultural and literary influence and transformation, a survey of how far later writers have strayed from Shakespeare's originals.

Verse

Creative responses to the Sonnets were slow to appear, partly due to the poems' omission from the First Folio. John Milton's (1608–74) 'An Epitaph on the Dramatic Poet W. Shakespeare', composed in 1630 and published at the forefront of the Second Folio of 1632, was his first poem to appear in print. It consists of sixteen lines of eight rhyming couplets and, in seeking to memorialize Shakespeare, shares some thematic and verbal resonance with Sonnet 55 ('Not marble, nor the gilded monuments | Of princes shall outlive this powerful rhyme', ll. 1–2) with the claim that Shakespeare's poetry, by pressing itself upon its readers' hearts and minds, 'Dost make us marble with too much conceiving'. Later, Milton's great sonnet 'When I consider how my light is spent' (1652?) echoes the opening of Shakespeare's Sonnets 12 and 64 with the dramatic proposition 'When I', and especially Sonnet 15 'When I consider everything that grows' in its praise for the transitory perfection of passing moments.

Edmond Malone's edition of the Sonnets did much to establish their reputation (see Chapter 9, above) and provided the necessary prologue for the Romantic writers' consequent engagement with them (see Chapter 10, above). John Keats's 'Sonnet written on a Blank Page in Shakespeare's Poems' (1819?) evokes Shakespeare's Sonnets 7, 15, and 116 in its consideration of the stars as symbols of constancy and silent witness. Its reference to the 'Bright star... in lone splendour hung aloft the night' echoes Shakespeare's Sonnet 27 in imagining the lover 'like a jewel (hung in ghastly night)' (l. 9). Keats's description of 'The moving waters at their priest-like task | Of pure ablution round earth's human shores' is reminiscent of the waves breaking against the shore in Sonnet 60, and his reference to 'my fair love's ripening breast' is similar to Sonnet 110's 'most, most loving breast' (l. 14). These last two possible allusions are made more compelling by Keats's having written the sonnet in a copy of Shakespeare's poems. Samuel Taylor Coleridge, helped by Charles Lamb, chose the sonnet as the most appropriate verse form in which to pay tribute to the great Shakespearian actress Sarah Siddons (1755–1831):

> As when a child on some long winter's night
> Affrighted clinging to its Grandam's knees,
> With eager wondering at the perturbed delight
> Listens strange tales of fearful dark decrees
> Muttered to wretch by necromantic spell;
> Or of those hags, who at the witching time
> Of murky midnight ride the air sublime,
> And mingle foul embrace with fiends of Hell.
> Cold Horror drinks its blood! Anon the tear
> More gentle starts, to hear the Beldame tell
> Of pretty babes, that loved each other dear,
> Murdered by cruel Uncle's mandate fell:
>   Ev'n such the shivering joys thy tones impart,
>   Ev'n so thou, Siddons! Meltest my sad heart.

Lady Macbeth was Siddons's greatest role, and Lamb's sonnet resonates with both *Macbeth* and *Richard III*, rather than with the Sonnets themselves, but his explicit use of a Shakespearian form for his praise shows how the sonnet was quickly becoming a shorthand way of establishing a context in which to write about and respond to Shakespeare. Later, Oscar Wilde was to write sonnets—'Portia' and 'Queen Henrietta Maria'—in praise of another great Shakespearian actress, Ellen Terry.

In a similar way to Coleridge and Lamb, Robert Southey's sonnet 6 (written in 1791) from *Poems on the Slave Trade* (1797–1810) takes from *Macbeth* a verbal allusion and adapts it (compare *Macbeth*, 1.7.19–20) for the closing couplet:

> Murder is legalized, that there the slave
> Before the Eternal, 'thunder-tongued shall plead
> Against the deep damnation of your deed.'

By surprising the reader with its Shakespearian authority in this way, Southey's sonnet at the same time reaffirms Shakespeare's supremacy as a writer of sonnets. Matthew Arnold and Henry Wadsworth Longfellow would assume the same with their sonnets about Shakespeare some years later. In 'Shakespeare' (Arnold, 1849; see p. 137, above) and 'A vision as of crowded city streets' (Longfellow, 1875) both poets choose the sonnet as the most appropriate poetic form to express admiration for Shakespeare.

One of the earliest (1872) and fullest reappropriations of a Shakespeare sonnet (No. 71) is Christina Rossetti's

> Remember me when I am gone away,
> Gone far away into the silent land;
> When you can no more hold me by the hand
> Nor I half turn to go yet turning stay.
> Remember me when no more day by day
> You tell me of our future that you planned:
> Only remember me; you understand
> It will be late to counsel then or pray.
> Yet if you should forget me for a while
> And afterwards remember, do not grieve:
> For if the darkness and corruption leave
> A vestige of the thoughts that once I had,

> Better by far you should forget and smile
> Than that you should remember and be sad.

The gentle but all-pervasive insistence that the beloved should remember the departed with words of the Ghost in *Hamlet*, 'Remember me' (1.5.91; compare 'remember thee', Sonnet 122, l. 13), is gradually relinquished, so that by the end of the sonnet the poet allows the beloved space for memory to be changed by Time, even into a happier forgetfulness. The sentiment that Rossetti reworks is to be found at the heart of Shakespeare's own sonnet:

> for I love you so
> That I in your sweet thoughts would be forgot,
> If thinking on me then should make you woe.
> (Sonnet 71, ll. 6–8)

Sonnet 71 is no less insistent, but Shakespeare emphasizes rather a self-pitying command to be forgotten, a negation which actually serves to underpin the memory it ostensibly seeks to erase, making his portrayal of the inevitability of forgetting more direct: 'let your love even with my life decay'. Both sonnets also evoke something of the physical nature of the poet's hands. Rossetti recalls the sensation of the poet and the beloved holding hands; Shakespeare asks the beloved not to remember 'the hand that writ' the poem in front of them. It seems unlikely that the addressees of these sonnets would forget for a moment the warm touch of the poet, however strong the encouragement might be to do so.

The joining of the poet's and beloved's hands is also evoked to powerful effect in the Shakespearian context of Alfred Tennyson's *In Memoriam A.H.H.*, a series of 132 lyrics of varying length written over a seventeen-year period (1833–50). As a collection the poems trace Tennyson reacting to the death of his friend, Arthur Hallam. The bleak emptiness of lyric 7 recalls 'a hand that can be clasp'd no more' (l. 5). In lyric 80, Tennyson is yearning for the ghost of Hallam to 'Reach out dead hands and comfort me' (l. 16). By the time he reaches lyric 119, Tennyson seems spiritually at one with the memory of his friend and is able to 'take the pressure of thine hand' (l. 12). Hallam's father's diffidence in relation to the Sonnets is mentioned in Chapter 10, above. Tennyson's sonnet 'If I were loved, as I desire to be' portrays the sensations of love unrequited and imagines the triumph of the lovers set apart from the world, whilst once again invoking the physical touch of hands and a pervasive homoeroticism: "Twere joy, not fear, clasped hand in hand with thee.' To consider *In Memoriam* as a collection of intimate, sexually ambiguous poems explicitly inspired by a male addressee provides a compelling context in which Tennyson's elegiac epic becomes the first substantial literary heir of Shakespeare's sonnets. Shakespeare was probably composing almost all his sonnets over a length of time (eighteen years, 1591–1609) similar to that which Tennyson took to produce the lyrics that became *In Memoriam*. Yet Shakespeare introduces the sense of a three-year period at various places in the collection. The three references to April in the Sonnets: Nos. 21, 98, and 104 (which also mention three winters, springs, autumns, and 'three hot Junes') help to establish an imaginary time frame. Similarly, Tennyson also employs a fictional three-year period, but is more systematic in this than Shakespeare, and uses it to frame the progression of his grief. *In Memoriam* mentions three Christmases which progressively fall 'sadly', 'calmly', and 'strangely' (lyrics 30, 78, and 105). As his grief develops into a deep, joyful calm, Tennyson's world becomes one of April (lyrics 115 and 116). An extraordinarily direct and brave connection is made with the Sonnets when Tennyson writes in lyric 61:

> I loved thee, Spirit, and love, nor can
> The soul of Shakespeare love thee more.
>
> (ll. 11–12)

The reference is brave because Shakespeare is here highlighted as the greatest love poet, a superlative assumption which interweaves by association all of Shakespeare's lovers, and kinds of loving, throughout *In Memoriam* itself and which implies that Tennyson loved Arthur Hallam in the same ways. Gregory Woods suggests that Tennyson may be trying to 'capitalise on patriotic defences of Shakespeare' but also sees Tennyson's cross-referral as a 'search for an acceptably unforeign precedent for extreme feelings of bliss generated by male love'.[2] Whether Tennyson intended to evoke the poetic voice of same-sex attraction to be found in Shakespeare's sonnets or not, his mentioning Shakespeare's loving has helped to make *In Memoriam* very much an exploration of masculine love, a love inextricably associated with Shakespeare's sonnets.[3]

Four more examples from the nineteenth century will serve to illustrate the diversity of the Sonnets' verbal echoes. Emily Brontë's ode 'To Imagination' (1844) opens with what might be considered as a reworking of Sonnets 27 and 29:

> When weary with the long day's care,
> And earthly change from pain to pain,
> And lost, and ready to despair,
> Thy kind voice calls me back again -
>   O my true friend, I am not lone
>   Whilst thou canst speak with such a tone!

Like the poetic voice in Sonnet 27, Emily Brontë's speaker is physically tired but mentally active and experiences a similar 'imaginary sight', a solace which arises when, like the poetic voice of Sonnet 29 (l. 9), she is 'in these thoughts [herself] almost despising'. Later, her imagination brings her 'hovering visions' and whispers 'with a voice divine | Of real worlds as bright as thine' (ll. 29–30). This is close to the lark ascending to sing 'hymns at heaven's gate' in Sonnet 29 (ll. 11–12); the inevitability of her experiencing such imaginings 'Yet still in evening's quiet hour | With never-failing thankfulness' (ll. 32–3), is comparable to the end of Sonnet 27:

> Lo, thus by day my limbs, by night my mind,
> For thee, and for myself, no quiet find.

The American poet and novelist Herman Melville (1819–91) (author of *Moby Dick*), in his sonnet 'Misgivings' (1860), presents a catalogue of apocalyptic occurrences of 'Nature's dark side'. There are a crashing spire, a flooded valley and 'torrents down the gorges go' (l. 12). The opening, 'When ocean-clouds over inland hills' and line 6, 'The tempest bursting from the waste of Time' echo the beginnings of Sonnet 106 ('the chronicle of wasted time') and Sonnet 12, line 10 ('the wastes of time'). The inventory format calls to mind Sonnet 66 and the Fool's prophecy in *The Tragedy of King Lear* (3.2.79–96). Similarly, Thomas Hardy's (1840–1928) 'When you shall see me in the toils of Time' (1866) evokes Sonnet 106, but considers the ravages of time from the female perspective:

My lauded beauties carried off from me,
My eyes no longer stars as in their prime,
My name forgot of Maiden Fair and Free...

The second poem in Algernon Charles Swinburne's (1837–1909) four-sonnet sequence 'Hermaphroditus' (1866) is concerned with the impossibility of love for a figure who is neither male nor female. Although the poetic voice of Shakespeare's Sonnet 144 is caught up in a love triangle, at least the underpinning dynamic is one of potential physical sex:

The better angel is a man right fair;
The worser spirit a woman coloured ill.
(Sonnet 144, ll. 3–4)

Swinburne's sonnet instead presents two negative illustrations:

But on the one side sat a man like death,
And on the other a woman sat like sin.
('Hermaphroditus', ll. 11–12)

The reminder of Sonnet 144's 'comfort and despair' (l. 1) actually becomes a desirable alternative to Swinburne's description:

Sex to sweet sex with lips and limbs is wed,
Turning the fruitful feud of hers and his
To the waste wedlock of a sterile kiss.
('Hermaphroditus', ll. 17–19)

Shakespeare's collection presents an abundant freedom of sexuality, even one that can love men and women at the same time. In contrast, for Swinburne's speaker, this same kind of sexuality, when represented in the body of one individual, leads to despair: 'Love turned himself and would not enter in' (l. 14).

Two sonnets by the great First World War poet Wilfred Owen (1893–1918) take the afterlife of Shakespeare's sonnets into the twentieth century. Wilfred Owen transcribed Sonnet 104 into his notebook and his sonnet 'With an identity disc' (1917) shows the influence of several others. A British soldier was issued with three identity discs, one of which was returned to his next of kin, if he was killed. 'Wear it, sweet friend' (l. 12), recalls the 'sweet love' of Shakespeare's Sonnets 76 and 79. The final lines

> Inscribe no date nor deed.
> But let thy heart-beat kiss it night and day,
> Until the name grow vague and wear away

recall 'Do not so much as my poor name rehearse; | But let your love even with my life decay' (Sonnet 71, ll. 11–12), as well as 'Thy sweet belovèd name no more shall dwell' (Sonnet 89, l. 10). The beating of the belovèd's/friend's heart touching the inscribed identity disc worn around the neck is rather like Shakespeare's lover being made present 'Where breath most breathes, even in the mouths of men' (Sonnet 81, l. 14).

Owen's 'How do I love thee?' (1917) glances back specifically to Elizabeth Barrett Browning's great love sonnet 'How do I love thee? Let me count the ways', yet Owen also finds a way of glancing back further to Shakespeare's sonnets. In 'How do I love thee?' Owen achieves a duality of reappropriation. Barrett Browning's celebration might be there in its title, but Shakespeare's is there more definitely to imply a forbidden, same-sex love:

> I cannot woo thee as the lion his mate,
> With proud parade and fierce prestige of presence;
> Nor thy fleet fancy may I captivate
> With pastoral attitudes in flowery pleasance;
> Nor will I kneeling court with thee sedate
> And comfortable plans of husbandhood;
> Nor file before thee as a candidate. . . .
> I cannot love thee as a lover would.
>
> To wrest thy hand from rivals, iron-gloved,
> Or cheat them by a craft, I am not clever.
> But I do love thee even as Shakespeare loved,
> Most gently wild and desperately for ever,
> Full-hearted, grave, and manfully in vain,
> With thought, high pain, and ever vaster pain.

The explicit mention of Shakespeare of course also opens up a dialogue between Owen's sonnet and Tennyson's *In Memoriam* (see pp. 148–50, above) and provides a double perspective on the poetry of same-sex desire. In its lines of negation (beginning 'Nor'), Owen's sonnet calls to mind Shakespeare's Sonnet 57 ('Being your slave, what should I do but tend | Upon the hours and times of your desire?', ll. 1–2). As in Sonnet 57, Owen's poetic voice is a slave to love though, unlike the voice in Sonnet 57, it remains painfully without irony. Sonnet 141, beginning in a similar fashion to Owen's ('In faith I do not love thee with mine eyes'), also includes comparable lines of negation:

> Nor are mine ears with thy tongue's tune delighted,
> Nor tender feeling to base touches prone,
> Nor taste, nor smell, desire to be invited
> To any sensual feast with thee alone.
>
> (Sonnet 141; ll. 5–8)

The crucial difference is that Owen's speaker implies that he would be only too pleased with all of these delights, if they were possible. Sonnet 141 also ends with the 'sin [that] awards me pain'; for Owen that pain is even greater. His reference to Shakespeare's loving being 'gently wild' could refer to Sonnet 102 and the song of the nightingale's 'wild music [that] burdens every bough' (l. 11). Keats's nightingale also sings in the air around Owen's sonnet, the adjective 'full-hearted' being like 'full-throated' in 'Ode to a Nightingale' (l. 10). Keats, Owen's other muse, helps to make more apparent the change of Philomel (Sonnet 102, l. 7) and emphasizes that the tragedy for Owen's speaker is that his particular way of loving will never requite the longing that he feels, will never change, but will remain the same 'desperately for ever'. Owen's poetic voice finds in Shakespeare's sonnet not only a complete, 'grave', and intellectual love, but the love of someone who desires his own sex 'manfully in vain, | With thought, high pain, and ever vaster pain.'

There is at least one further duality in those last lines. They refer to ever-living longing and could also allude to sodomy, painful if it takes place as rape, and this itself would explain the suppressed Ovidian nightingale present in Owen's own, and by implication in Shakespeare's, 'wild music'.

There is a buried sonnet in T. S. Eliot's 'The Waste Land' (1922), well disguised by the beguiling and seductive rhyme schemes deployed in 'The Fire Sermon' (ll. 173–265). Significantly, it completes the prophecy of Tiresias. The structure is Shakespearian and the lines work well out of context:

> The time is now propitious, as he guesses,
> The meal is ended, she is bored and tired,
> Endeavours to engage her in caresses
> Which still are unreproved, if undesired.
> Flushed and decided, he assaults at once;
> Exploring hands encounter no defence;
> His vanity requires no response,
> And makes a welcome of indifference.
> (And I Tiresias have foresuffered all
> Enacted on this same divan or bed;
> I who have sat by Thebes below the wall
> And walked among the lowest of the dead.)
> Bestows one final patronising kiss,
> And gropes his way, finding the stairs unlit...

After the sex, there are more gropes and a sense of love being sullied, conveyed by the closing, half-rhyming, couplet. There is even a suggestion of Lucrece-like violation: 'Flushed and decided, he assaults at once; | Exploring hands encounter no defence'. The context for Eliot's use of the sonnet form is well established by other Shakespearian allusions in 'The Waste Land'. The folly of lust rather than love makes it comparable to sonnets in the later part of Shakespeare's collection.

Finally, moving swiftly to the other end of the twentieth century—but pausing to notice W. H. Auden's (1907–73) 'Our Bias' (1940), which in its opening line, 'The hour-glass whispers to the lion's paw', echoes the beginning of Sonnet 19 ('Devouring Time, blunt thou the lion's paws', making it a Shakespearian-like exploration of the effects of time)—there is the comic and whimsical poetry of Wendy Cope (b. 1945). Her spoof sonnet sequence 'Strugnell's Sonnets' in *Making Cocoa for Kingsley Amis* (1986) gently mocks several of Shakespeare's poems and illustrates their afterlife in the ironic climate of postmodernity. Here is her reworking of Sonnets 55, 64, and 66:

> Not only marble, but the plastic toys
> From cornflake packets will outlive this rhyme:
> I can't immortalize you, love—our joys
> Will lie unnoticed in the vault of time.

When Mrs Thatcher has been cast in bronze
And her administration is a page
In some O-level text-book, when the dons
Have analysed the story of our age,
When travel firms sell tours of outer space
And aeroplanes take off without a sound
And Tulse Hill has become a trendy place
And Upper Norwood's on the underground
    Your beauty and my name will be forgotten-
    My love is true, but all my verse is rotten.

Cope's is a Shakespearian sonnet in its form, the humour of which relies on the reputation of Shakespeare's sonnets and on their hyperbolic claims being sufficiently known in order to be overturned by her litotes drawn from the popular culture of the 1980s. Her use of proper names might imply that she is prompting the reader to consider Shakespeare's sonnets biographically, too. That it should come to this!

Prose

One of the first pieces of creative criticism in prose thoroughly to engage with Shakespeare's sonnets was Oscar Wilde's *A Portrait of Mr W.H.* (see Chapter 10, above). Since then novelists especially have referred closely to the Sonnets during the course of their narratives and continue to do so. As well as celebrating the literary qualities of the poems, the tendency is to write new fantasies usually inspired by the quest to read the Sonnets biographically and to focus upon aspects of their sexuality and psychology. What follows are just a few representative examples.

Marcel Proust's (1871–1922) *A la recherche du temps perdu* (1913–27) has long been associated with the Sonnets, mainly because of the English translation by C. K. Scott-Montcrieff, the title of which directly alludes to Sonnet 30: 'the remembrance of things past'. The allusion to the sonnet is only possible with the English translation of the title which makes it difficult to disassociate Proust from Shakespeare, and Shakespeare's Sonnet 30 from Proust's great achievement. The novel is circular in construction, ending where it begins, irrevocably referring the reader back to the experience of the past. Whilst Shakespeare's poetic voice goes on a journey of consolation through Sonnet 30, it is clear that 'sessions of sweet silent thought' will occur again after 'losses are restored'. Proust's novel and Shakespeare's Sonnets both represent struggles against the destructive nature of Time and evoke myriad particularities of human perception and relationships as they do so.

A more specific but no less elegiac relationship with the Sonnets is drawn directly in Virginia Woolf's *To The Lighthouse* (1927). In the strained silence that exists between Mr and Mrs Ramsey, as they both read, towards the end of the novel's first section, 'The Window', they observe one another and attempt to guess what each other is thinking and feeling, Mrs Ramsey comes across Sonnet 98:

She was climbing up those branches, this way and that, laying hands on one flower and then another.

'Nor praise the deep vermilion in the rose', she read, and so reading she was ascending, she felt, on the top, on to the summit. How satisfying! How restful! All the odds and ends of the day stuck to this magnet; her mind felt swept, felt clean. And then there it was, suddenly entire; she held it in her hands, beautiful and reasonable, clear and complete, the essence sucked out of life and rounded here—the sonnet.

Mrs Ramsey's physical sensations, her 'ascending', again call to mind that famous 'lark at break of day arising' (Sonnet 29, l. 11) and her arrival at the summit recalls 'Now stand you on the top of happy hours' (Sonnet 16, l. 5). Her reaction to Sonnet 98, a sonnet of absence, searching, and longing, calls to mind the events of her day and orders her own sense of autobiography. Shakespeare's Sonnets here represent life distilled and comprehended as they provide solace for Mrs Ramsey. Woolf explicitly privileges the female with this outlook; the male can only look on ignorantly as Mrs Ramsey continues to read and is empowered by Sonnet 98 to break the silence between them:

He wondered if she understood what she was reading. Probably not, he thought. She was astonishingly beautiful. Her beauty seemed to him, if it were possible, to increase
Yet seem'd it winter still, and, you away,

As with your shadow I with these did play,
she finished.
'Well?' she said, echoing his smile dreamily, looking up from her book.
As with your shadow I with these did play,
she murmured, putting the book on the table.

Whilst reading a sonnet about absence, both Mr and Mrs Ramsey have been absent from each other in their respective reading. It is significant that, after putting down the Sonnets, Mrs Ramsey breaks the silence by telling her husband of the engagement between Paul Rayley and Minta Doyle. And it is this empowerment that Woolf grants Mrs Ramsey through the reading of Sonnet 98 that also makes her able to speak the words that she knows her husband wants to hear. She admits that it will rain tomorrow and by so doing 'she had triumphed again. She had not said it: yet he knew'. In her earlier novel, *Mrs Dalloway* (1925), Woolf describes how 'seriously and solemnly Richard Dalloway got on his hind legs and said that no decent man ought to read Shakespeare's Sonnets because it was like listening at keyholes (besides, the relationship was not one that he approved)'.[4] In *To the Lighthouse*, Woolf has a *decent woman* reading the Sonnets and in so doing invites the reader to listen at the keyhole of Mrs Ramsey's conscience, and to consider her marriage to Mr Ramsey—presumably a 'decent man'.

Anthony Burgess's novel *Nothing Like the Sun* (the title taken from Sonnet 130) was published on 23 April 1964 to help celebrate the four hundredth anniversary of Shakespeare's birth. Burgess adopts a highly original and creative diction through which to present this fictional, biographical exploration of Shakespeare's life. He employs much wordplay and many invented words, sexual metaphors, and Shakespearian allusions as the reader is consistently shown the world from Shakespeare's own point of view. The writing of sonnets is depicted as being natural and important to Shakespeare from his boyhood, and Burgess provides several fictional examples of early and aborted or lost attempts. There are also suggestions of dark and black ladies throughout, which from their earliest mention are connected to a promiscuous, dissident, and self-castigating sexuality, for example: 'It was this one ready wench—black-eyed, the flue on her body black, her hair black and shining as blackbirds that fed on thrown-out bacon fat—but it might too have been Bess, Joan, Meg, Susan, Kate'.[5] These women contrast starkly with Anne Hathaway, who is described as 'fair and English, smelling of mild summers and fresh water' (Burgess, p. 29). Later, Shakespeare watches a dark-coloured prostitute at work:

The woman was black, shining, naked, agape, thrust against the wall as though at bay [an allusion to Sonnet 137, l. 6?], and there rammed and rammed at her a bulky seaman, in unbuttoned shirt and points loosened for his work...She pulled her gown swiftly down further from her shoulders, disclosing nipples black as ink-blobs; she came for him smiling, her arms held out. (pp. 58–9)

Years later, Shakespeare encounters another 'dark lady', 'brown not Negro' (p. 145), with whom he has an affair which is recounted as a series of journal entries in 1596 (the affair proper starts on Hamnet and Judith Shakespeare's birthday, 2 February). Burgess alludes progressively to the lust of Sonnet 129 (as well as to *Hamlet*, 1.2.144–5 in 'the act growing with the act of feeding'):

But I possess her in a terrible joy, the appetite growing with the act of feeding, which astonishes me. And in the end I coldly see that I have a mistress. And a very rare one...And after, in a cold and rainy May evening, I sit in mine own lodgings feeling truly in a wretched dim hell of mine own making, spent, used, shameless, shameful. (pp. 150 and 155)

His mistress's name is Fatima, meaning 'Destiny'. This nomenclature is discussed in the 1982 foreword and relates to the acrostic riddle that Burgess includes in the novel's dedication, based on Sonnet 147. Henry Wriothesley also appears at various points in the novel. He is presented neatly as Mr W.H. when he describes his practice of placing the initial of his family name before his first name. Burgess's Shakespeare clearly adores this Earl of Southampton and writes him sonnets (notably Sonnet 20), 'it was true, it was a woman's beauty, but there was the swooning delight of its being on no woman's body' (pp. 106–7). To complicate both biography and fiction and to frustrate any single, definite interpretation of the Sonnets that may be gleaned from the novel, Mr W.H., too, has a dark mistress, 'black-haired and black-eyed' (p. 116). Racing towards his conclusion, Burgess has Anne suspecting William of an affair, because of a sonnet of his given to her by Richard Quiney, and Shakespeare discovering Anne in bed with Richard. Fatima declares that she has given birth to Shakespeare's illegitimate son, a final pun on the novel's title.

The possibility of another illegitimate child by Shakespeare occurs in Erica Jong's *Serenissima* (1987), a biographical fantasia inspired by the Sonnets, and set in Venice. Jessica Pruitt, the novel's heroine, is a world-famous Hollywood actress whose passion for Shakespeare is realized literally when she slips back in time to sixteenth-century Venice. She meets and has sex with both Shakespeare and the Earl of Southampton. Unwittingly she becomes the biographical coincidence behind the real Jessica in *The Merchant of Venice* (a young Jew and fictional candidate for the Dark Ladyship) whose father Shalach is the inspiration for Shylock.

From the first, the labyrinth of Venice, which J. A. Symonds referred to as the 'Shakespeare of cities, unchallenged, incomparable, and beyond envy',[6] becomes a powerful metaphor for self-reflection, the complications of love and the Sonnets themselves: 'It is not surprising that Venice is known above all for mirrors and glass since Venice is the most narcissistic city in the world, the city that celebrates self-mirroring'.[7] Recalling her childhood, the narrator uses the intriguing word 'cryptosexual' (unknown to the *Oxford English Dictionary*) to describe her early journals; Sonnets 61, 57, 129, 42, 135, and 19 are quoted in full as an important, though cryptic, part of *Serenissima*'s narrative. Allusions to other sonnets occur throughout the novel and some of its fourteen chapters are also headed with direct quotations, for example: 'In War With Time' (chapter 6; Sonnet 15), 'Beauty's Doom' (chapter 12; Sonnet 14), and 'Hell of Time' (chapter 14; Sonnet 120).

The story is also Shakespeare's, though, and much is made of the biographical appeal of the Sonnets:

If you read the sonnets carefully, the pain is unmistakable. This was a man who loved and was betrayed. This was a man who was hurt to his heart's very quick. Whoever the 'straying youth' he loved, there is no question that he loved an arrogant narcissist and that he himself was the unrequited lover, not the beloved. The ache is *in* the sonnets. It is palpable. It is most palpable, in fact, when the poet most tries to rationalize himself out of it. (Jong, p. 80)

From this apprehension of vulnerability comes the assumption and expectation, present throughout *Serenissima*, that Shakespeare is the most lustful and at the same time the most expert and sensitive of lovers. Jong is able to play wittily with fictional deferral. If anyone could describe what it might be like to have sex with Shakespeare, Jong could. Frustratingly, she refrains: 'After all, who would dare describe love with the greatest poet the world has ever known, the poet who himself defined love?' (p. 165). Henry Wriothesley appears as effeminate in appearance and his explicitly bisexual preferences lead on to an interpretation of the last two lines of Sonnet 20:

Will knows that this is part of his contract with Harry, to be a player-playmate, to share a woman between the two of them so as to disguise Harry's preference for the double-pricked pleasure of man on man, the passion of the master who is also a mistress, a master-mistress, so to say. (p. 114)

Here Jong engages with the love triangle often perceived in the Sonnets, and she reiterates the fantastic elements of it throughout her novel.

Finally, an early twenty-first-century attempt to novelize the Sonnets is Lennard J. Davis's *The Sonnets: A Novel* (2001). The narrator, Will Marlow (combining the names of Shakespeare and Christopher Marlowe), is a modern English professor at Columbia University whose life and loves assume a striking resemblance to Shakespeare's. A quotation from the Sonnets provides the name for each of the eighteen chapters. There are descriptions of seminars on the Sonnets in chapters 5 and 10. These are both parodic as well as genuinely discursive. Davis's is a self-consciously witty, thinly written novel and includes several heavy-handed allusions to the Sonnets, for example: 'I looked at the clock and saw that the day was sunk into night' (Sonnet 12) and 'I was alone beweeping my outcast state when the phone rang' (Sonnet 29).[8] Defensively reaffirming his heterosexual identity, the narrator falls for an effeminate 'master-mistress' male student, Christopher Johnson (combining the names of Christopher Marlowe and Jonson), 'not exactly a girl, but like a girl'.[9] Marlow has a disastrous affair with one of his female students, a 'dark lady' (Greek, Middle Eastern, French, Jewish), Chantal S. T. Mukarjee. The affair leads to a separation between Will Marlow and his wife, Anne (named after Anne Hathaway). Unlike the novels by Burgess and Jong, Davis's stays in the present, but permits one flight of fantasy when Marlow imagines himself as Shakespeare returning to his wife in Stratford-upon-Avon. Marlow goes on to discover the joys of gay love and is 'never happier in [his] life' than when he finally gets to have sex with Christopher Johnson, which completely ends his marriage, and the novel.

Drama

Three American dramatic works which appeared at almost the same time all relate to the Sonnets in different ways. The first, *Love's Fire* (1998), engages with the content of the Sonnets and is a collection of seven short plays by American playwrights (Eric Bogosian: Sonnet 118; William Finn: Sonnet 102; John Guare: Sonnets 153 and 154; Tony Kushner: Sonnet 75; Marsha Norman: Sonnet 140; Ntozake Shange: Sonnet 128; and Wendy Wasserstein: Sonnet 94). The plays are intended to be performed as a collection and, like the Sonnets themselves, each individual play takes on a heightened and different meaning when considered in its wider context. Mark Lamos's introduction to the volume interestingly assumes that Shakespeare's sonnets, unlike those embedded in his plays, were never meant to be read out loud, but were:

designed to be read quietly by candle light or natural daylight—especially if they were delivered to a chosen recipient. That proved to be one of the challenges of *Love's Fire*: incorporating these sonnets spoken by the actors into seven plays whose language is startlingly contemporary.[10]

The plays in *Love's Fire* are varied in thematic and dramatic scope and each concludes with a cast member reading the sonnet which inspired it. 'Bitter Sauce' by Eric Bogosian explores what happens when one partner seeks infidelity with a totally different kind of lover, making a metaphorical parallel with the lines in Sonnet 118:

> Even so, being full of your ne'er-cloying sweetness,
> To bitter sauces did I frame my feeding.

> (ll. 5–6)

Bogosian adopts a contemporary diction through the use of slang and expletives. The unfaithful Rengin explains to the bewildered Herman:

I was in this bar one night, getting shit-faced because I was so in love with you
and it felt so weird and I, well, I figured the best antidote to how intense our
love was, was something just as intense, but in the other direction. (*Love's Fire*,
p. 10)

And so she starts a relationship built entirely on lust with the
biker, Red. Marsha Norman's title-less play is an amusing visual
depiction of promiscuity based on Sonnet 140 and especially the
lines:

> Now this ill-wresting world is grown so bad,
> Mad slanderers by mad ears believed be.
>   That I may not be so, nor thou belied,
>   Bear thine eyes straight, though thy proud heart go wide.
>
> (ll. 11–14)

So, the audience sees a series of couples meet and separate into new
partnerships while their original lovers remain present as onstage
witnesses. Hence, in a variety of sexual relationships there is Wife,
David, Jackie, Roland, Roland's New Lover (male), Roland's Lover's
New Lover (female), Roland's New Lover's Lover (male). At the end
of the sequence, this final character starts a new relationship with the
original Wife.

Tony Kushner's play *Terminating, or Lass Meine Schmerzen Nicht
Verloren Sein, or Ambivalence* presents two mutual dialogues in parallel:
Esther and her lesbian lover Dymphna and Hendryk, and his gay
lover, Billygoat. Esther is psychoanalysing Hendryk, who makes occasional sexual propositions to her. Kushner takes pains to have Billygoat speak lines directly from Sonnet 75 during the course of the
drama which serves to disrupt the flow of modern dialogue. Kushner's
dialogues explore the impossibility of love, suggesting that desire is
sometimes only one-directional and that human relationships often
compromise themselves accordingly. A moment of exasperation best
illustrates the different pathways of desire which Kushner depicts,
which is not only inspired by the Sonnets, but is reminiscent of *As You
Like It* (5.4.79–103). Human love is reduced to its most basic, and for
Kushner's characters most complex, instinct:

HENDRYK (*to Esther*) Can I fuck you?
DYMPHNA (*to Esther*) Can I fuck you?

BILLYGOAT (*to Hendryk*) Can I fuck you?

ESTHER (*to Hendryk*) No. (*To Dymphna*) No fucking tonight. (*Love's Fire*, p. 62)

As Dymphna observes towards the end: 'Our inability to love one another is humankind's greatest tragedy' (*Love's Fire*, p. 64), perhaps relating her crisis to Sonnet 75's couplet:

> Thus do I pine and surfeit day by day,
> Or gluttoning on all, or all away.

Though not infinite in its variety, *Love's Fire* presents several challenges to performers and is surely a fine testimony to the enduring power of the Sonnets to inspire modern writers. Its language is direct and uncompromising, and the scripts cry out to be performed in order to release the power of their modern diction, subtle effects of physical movement, and the theatrical pictures required by the stage directions.

Three of Shakespeare's sonnets are used in Joe Calarco's adaptation *Shakespeare's R & J* (1998), which retells *Romeo and Juliet* through the adolescent longings and sexual fascinations of four Roman Catholic schoolboys who read and perform the play together. This highly inventive and theatrically powerful reappropriation finds a repressive modern context in which to make new meanings from Shakespeare's tragedy and one which raises questions about the nature of forbidden love. The issue of homophobia is inevitably raised but, as Calarco explains in his introduction, his adaptation aims to extend beyond polemicism: 'This is a play about men. It is about how men interact with other men. Thus it deals with how men view women, sex, sexuality, and violence.'[11] To introduce and illustrate the obsessive nature of adolescent love Student 1 is seen writing love poems to his girlfriend at the beginning of the play and incidentally composes Sonnet 147: 'My love is as a fever, longing still'. This is followed immediately by the other three students making a prayer of penitence. Later, during *Romeo and Juliet*'s marriage scene, Students 3 and 4, perhaps out of homosexual jealousy or homophobia, take away the copy of *Romeo and Juliet* (from which the students occasionally read their parts) from Students 1 and 2 who are playing the roles. At a loss what to say, Student 1 starts speaking Sonnet 18 ('Shall I compare thee to a summer's day?') and gradually works through it with Student 2.

Students 3 and 4 continue to taunt them, but Shakespeare's sonnet is locked in their memories and nothing will stop them using it as an expression of imaginary and eternal commitment. After Student 3's frustration has led him to strike Student 1 across the face with the play-text, he immediately becomes penitent and starts reciting Sonnet 116: 'Let me not to the marriage of true minds | Admit impediments'. All the students join in and the sonnet becomes a clear affirmation of their reunion as friends, as well as an acknowledgement that in the story of *Romeo and Juliet* they have found a way of affirming all kinds of love, a way of being free.

The last example shows how the sonnet form is used to relate to the major concerns of a play. Anthony Burgess, on the last page of *Nothing Like the Sun*, alludes to words from John Donne's 'Death, thou shalt die' (*Holy Sonnets*, 6):[12] 'One short sleep past'. Margaret Edson's 1999 drama, *Wit* (made into a film directed by Mike Nichols, with Emma Thompson in the leading role), about Professor Vivian Bearing, a John Donne scholar, dying of cancer, includes a moment of flashback which serves as a piece of close criticism of the way a sonnet can be punctuated. Vivian remembers a particular tutorial on Donne's Holy Sonnet 6. The remarks of her tutor, 'the great E. M. Ashford', serve to emphasize how profoundly important the punctuation of just two lines of any sonnet can be:

Do you think the punctuation of the last line of this sonnet is merely an insignificant detail?
The sonnet begins with a valiant struggle with death, calling on the forces of intellect and drama to vanquish the enemy. But it is ultimately about over-coming the seemingly insuperable barriers separating life, death, and eternal life.
In the edition you chose, this profoundly simple meaning is sacrificed to hysterical punctuation:
'And Death—*capital D*—shall be no more—*semicolon!* Death—*capital D*—comma—thou shalt die—*exclamation point!*'
If you go in for this sort of thing, I suggest you take up Shakespeare.
[Helen] Gardner's edition of the Holy Sonnets returns to the Westmoreland manuscript source of 1610—not for sentimental reasons, I assure you, but because Helen Gardner is a *scholar*. It reads:
'And death shall be no more, *comma*, Death thou shalt die.'
(*As she recites this line, she makes a little gesture at the comma*)

Nothing but a breath—a comma—separates life from life everlasting. It is very simple really. With the original punctuation restored, death is no longer something to act out on a stage, with exclamation points. It's a comma, a pause.

This way, the *uncompromising* way, one learns something from this poem, wouldn't you say? Life, death. Soul, God. Past, present. Not insuperable barriers, not semicolons, just a comma.[13]

These observations are just as relevant to any reader of Shakespeare's sonnets as they are to Donne's. Choices about how to punctuate the Sonnets should neither be taken, nor read, lightly.

This brief survey of poetry, novels, and plays which engage with, and to some extent rewrite, Shakespeare's sonnets serves to illustrate how these 154 poems are forever being *un*finished by subsequent writers. The artistic re-creation that is brought to bear on the Sonnets can serve the immediate demands of a wide range of other narratives and forms. Whether these are biographical, psychological, elegiac, fantastic in their scope, explicitly literary, or concerned with issues of gender and sexuality, Shakespeare's sonnets are constantly being re-invented afresh in new contexts. A final comparison with Virginia Woolf's 1928 novel *Orlando* will serve to illustrate something of this ongoing potential of the Sonnets to inspire.

Orlando, born as a nobleman in the sixteenth century, one day transforms into a woman and travels, with effortless immortality, through all subsequent centuries. In Woolf's novel, Orlando is writing a poem, 'The Oak Tree', a powerful symbol of how his and her poetic voice changes and evolves through time. Shakespeare's sonnets, with their appeal and address to both sexes, and to the widest spectrum of human sexuality, continue, Orlando-like, to transcend time, themselves the objects of apparent universal interest and change. If we think we have exhausted their inexhaustibility it is we ourselves who are exhausted; if we think we have finished reading them, then it is time we turned to other writers to unfinish them for us.

The Sonnets in Performance

For those who do not believe that the Sonnets should only be read silently, many audio recordings are readily available either for purchase, or for consultation in library archives; many more exist among long-obscured and rare audio anthologies. Major recordings include Dame Edith Evans reading her own selection,[1] Sir John Gielgud (120 sonnets, Caedmon, 1963), Richard Pasco (complete, Argo, 1979), Alex Jennings (complete, Naxos, 1997), and a team made up of Brian Dennehy, Al Pacino, Natasha Richardson, Patrick Stewart, Kathleen Turner, and others (*The Complete Shakespeare Sonnets: Read by Outstanding Actors of the American and British Stage*, Airplay, 2000). The interpretative choices implicit in audio performances provide a further critical focus on the Sonnets' status as a collection of poems, as well as on their status as texts to be spoken aloud.

When heard, the emotional journey of the Sonnets can become differently inflected depending on the sex, age, and interests of the performer. A male or female voice will automatically determine the gender of Shakespeare's poetic persona and might serve to challenge a listener's assumptions about the nature of the collection. In sound recordings, irony becomes a quality that is determined to a greater or lesser extent and it becomes possible immediately to emphasize particular words and feelings as the reading progresses. Or, the performance might be most interested in the lyricism of the Sonnets; the focus might be on verse reading, elocution, and the sounds of words, rather than on a quest for successive articulations of emotional truth. How, if at all, is music used in a recording? Does this attempt to evoke the Renaissance period, or is it modern? The way the recording is received and used will vary immeasurably depending on whether it is in cassette or CD format. The former will make listening more likely to be a linear process; the latter might make it possible for the listener either randomly to select different tracks or easily to select which sonnets to hear. How far does a recording of the Sonnets assume that a reader will listen to it without following the printed poems in an edition? It is difficult to listen to more than a few at any one time without the Sonnets beginning to merge, especially if read by only one speaker, and the space which the words occupy as verse becomes invisible. A solo performance might raise questions about autobiographical interpretation and the collection could sound like scenes from the life of the same individual. Likewise, a multivocal recording, whilst offering welcome variation and vocal texture, might plot a specific narrative, biographical or otherwise, through the collection which could detract from the aural integrity of individual poems.

The 1958 British Council Argo recording by Cambridge University's Marlowe Society, directed by George 'Dadie' Rylands, uses ten different male voices to

ease the monotony which is inevitable if one is to listen to more than a hundred and fifty poems by one hand in a single and restricted form... This helps to emphasize different moods, to mark variations on a theme in the opening sequence, and suggest links and collocations. For instance Sonnets 71–74 which treat of the poet's imagined death have a grave melancholy of their own. And then sometimes the changes are abrupt. Sonnet 116 ('Let me not to the marriage of true minds') is immediately followed by 'Accuse me thus...', which strikes a more bitter and dramatic note which is sustained until Sonnet 122. Sonnet 18 demands a more youthful and romantic voice than those which have preceded it. The difference in age of the readers in fact covers a span of more than thirty years.[2]

Another more recent multivocal recording was directed by Peter Orr (who worked extensively with Rylands on the British Council Argo recordings of Shakespeare) for Penguin in 1995. Again, the voices used are exclusively male, but there are only four of them: Peter Egan (who reads 25 sonnets), Bob Peck (37), Michael Williams (51), and Orr himself (41). These unequal shares combine to establish various runs and clusters of poems, achieve a heightened effect of contrast, and make possible unusual relationships between the poems. For example,

Williams's reading of Sonnets 14–20 distorts any sense of the first seventeen poems forming a separate sequence about procreation. Similarly, Egan reads Sonnets 126 and 128, thus closely relating the two parts of the collection, which remain potentially distinct by Orr reading Sonnet 127. Thematically, the vocal variations contribute much to the recording. The early transition from Sonnet 3 (Egan) to Sonnet 4 (Williams) emphasizes the castigation of the self-consuming death of a narcissist ('Die single, and thine image dies with thee', Sonnet 3, l. 14) with a different voice: 'Unthrifty loveliness, why dost thou spend | Upon thyself thy beauty's legacy?' (Sonnet 4, ll. 1–2), and returns to the salutary warning tone of Sonnet 2, also read by Williams. Such manoeuvres are not as smooth or imperceptible as they might otherwise have been as each reader resolutely announces the number of the sonnet he is about to read, in critically distant, impartial tones. Orr does not speak until Sonnet 23, 'As an unperfect actor on the stage', which is probably a private joke. Unlike his company, Orr did not make his reputation primarily as a performer.

The Royal Academy of Dramatic Art celebrated Valentine's Day 2002 with Michael Kamen's audio recording for EMI, *When Love Speaks* (an allusion to *Love's Labour's Lost* 4.3.320). This CD is as much a celebration of RADA's distinguished alumni as it is a celebration of Shakespeare's sonnets and it offers many different interpretative perspectives and ways of reading. Forty-seven sonnets are selected, only nine of which are from the second part of the collection. The numeric ordering is substituted by a subjective and seemingly random arrangement. This recording is about matching different performers to a series of apparently disconnected poems. Twenty-nine men and fourteen women make up the company of sonnet readers. Juliet Stevenson reads Sonnet 128, Sylvia Syms Sonnet 141: both poems which are usually assumed to have female addressees. The recording includes many fine and intimate sounding examples of sonnet readings in a variety of styles, from John Gielgud's affirming but declamatory Sonnet 23 to Kenneth Branagh's heartbreaking, yet restrained, reading of Sonnet 30. Alan Rickman reads Sonnet 130 with complete seriousness, lacking even the slightest whiff of the crucial irony implicit in its verse. Four modern musical settings are also included: Sonnet 29 (Rufus Wainwright), Sonnet 35 (Keb' Mo'), Sonnet 18 (Bryan Ferry), and Sonnet 8 (Ladysmith Black Mambazo). The last is a rare example of a polyphonic performance of a single sonnet. Beginning with the line 'Mark how one string, sweet husband to another' (Sonnet 8, l. 9), the setting gradually turns into a chanted meditation on 'joy delights in joy' (l. 2), whilst a single voice sings the whole sonnet underneath it. Other Shakespeare songs, a speech set to music, and a setting of Christopher Marlowe's 'Come live with me and be my love' (sung by Annie Lennox) are interspersed among the sonnet performances.

Two contrasting single-voiced recordings are those made by Simon Callow and Alex Jennings. Callow performed the whole collection on stage in 1983. He used John Padel's 1982 sequence which reordered the poems according to his own complicated and fanciful numerological and biographical interests and the belief that William Herbert, the Earl of Pembroke, was Mr W.H. For Callow, preparing to perform the Sonnets was all-embracing and life-enhancing:

My identification with Shakespeare's emotional experience was total. It seemed to be my life he was writing down. The psychological realism was shocking and sometimes overwhelming.

He originally performed them in a series of three separate programmes, platform performances at the Royal National Theatre. On one occasion he performed all three shows in the same afternoon:

I was somewhat tired, my voice a little hoarse, and my nerves in shreds… I staggered onto the stage, my heart beating even faster than it might have done on account of the ten cups of black coffee which I'd drunk in the dressing room. I plunged into the first sonnet—and immediately fouled up a line… I'm ashamed to say I did not do Shakespeare's sonnets justice.[3]

Callow's audio recording twelve years later, whilst reverting to the 1609 ordering, commits no less of an injustice. He reads them quickly (on average about forty-eight seconds per sonnet) and gets through the whole collection in approximately two hours and twenty minutes. His intonation tends to suppress individual words at the expense of variety, drama, and texture and gives his reading the overall effect of an elocutionary exercise. In its favour, Callow's recording does not include the numbers of each sonnet. Alex Jennings does number them in his recording, crisply differentiating one from another. His delivery is slower (on average about sixty-four seconds per sonnet) and is set apart from other modern recordings in that the listener never forgets for a moment that Jennings is reading from a script. This choice of a highly controlled and restrained delivery evokes something of the discipline of the sonnet form. Jennings allows for the individuality and sound of each poem to shine through his reading of it, and for Shakespeare's words to attain a level of ambiguity so that the listeners can locate the Sonnets' meaning. Different possibilities remain open thanks to Jennings's admirable restraint.

Sonnets on Stage and Screen

The Sonnets have been adapted many times and in many forms for stage productions. What follows is just a handful of recent examples. *Sweet Sessions* (1991), taking its title from Sonnet 30, was devised by Paul Godfrey and Nancy Meckler for Shared Experience. The production drew a sharp distinction between academia and poetry, between the Academy and Theatre. The central figure of a female Ph.D. student working on the Sonnets, and busily indexing their imagery, was surrounded by the figures of Shakespeare, the Dark Lady, and the Young Man, who challenged her knowledge of the poems and illustrated relationships within the collection through performance. One critic recalls 'at one point the student in a fit of undergraduate feminism shouted at Shakespeare for not allowing the Dark Lady any voice of her own'.[4]

In 1992, a Welsh theatre company, Volcano, produced a controversial piece of aggressively physical theatre inspired by the Sonnets. *L.O.V.E.* took as its premiss a *ménage à trois* of two men and one woman (with three chairs and a bed) to explore the potential violence which the Sonnets contain in contradiction to their formal appearance. Directed by Nigel Charnock (of the dance group DV8), the show included many acrobatics, an erotic wrestling-match version of Sonnet 18, and at one point had the woman pulling a knife from her bunch of roses and threatening to castrate the two men. The rhythm of the Sonnets helped to determine physical movement, especially the lines: 'perjured, murd'rous, bloody, full of blame, | Savage, extreme, rude, cruel, not to trust' (Sonnet 129, lines 3–4), which were repeated in the form of a verbal attack. Even Shirley Bassey was invoked as one of the men lip-synched her version of the song 'Something' (originally composed by George Harrison). Here is a postmodern example of a voice which puts into circulation notions of straight and gay love with varying degrees of histrionicism and irony. The show was revived in 2003 and chosen to tour in celebration of ten years of the British Council's presence in Georgia. It was greeted with protests from the director and actors of Tbilisi's Marjanishvili Theatre when performed there, as well as from the Georgian Orthodox Church. The Volcano company received anonymous threats of vandalism and was forced to cancel its two remaining shows.

In recent years, an Amsterdam stand-up comedian, William Sutton, who is also a Shakespeare scholar, has explored his obsession with the Sonnets and created his own one-man Sonnet show. It took him four years to learn the collection by heart and audiences at the Edinburgh Fringe Festival in 2002 were not only able to call out random numbers between 1 and 154, and hear the appropriate sonnet, but could challenge Sutton with a single line, phrase, and in some instances word, whereupon he would perform the correct sonnet back to them. His working knowledge of the poems is only possible through a dedicated method of aural saturation and a constant drive to call to mind any poem in the collection at random. His show, which presents imaginative ways of thinking about the poems, has also been warmly received at schools around the world.

In 1985, the gay film director Derek Jarman made a seventy-eight-minute film inspired by the Sonnets, *The Angelic Conversation*. An epigraph declares that 'Love is too young to know what conscience is, | Yet who knows not conscience is born of love?' (Sonnet 151, ll. 1–2). This odd and haunting film runs at three frames per second, enlarged from 35 mm film, showing images of two men in various physical activities: carrying logs and flame torches, walking through rocky landscapes (in what seems to be an island location), climbing, waiting, swimming, and ultimately making love. At one point there is a weird sequence, shot at usual speed, of what appears to be a mysterious ceremonial washing and dressing of another man with bystanders. The effect of the cinematography (a washed-out colour effect that explores subtle gradations of shade) is strangely hypnotic and meditative. Judi Dench reads fourteen sonnets in a slightly echoic voice-over: Sonnets 57 (without its couplet), 90, 43, 53, 148 (usually assumed to be addressed to a woman), 126 (which immediately succeeds 148), 29, 94, 30, 55, 27, 61, 56, and 104. Some of the film images and sounds invite the viewer to make connections between them: the fire-torch, the reflecting sun-like disc, the use of room interiors, and the sound of waves. Most of the music is by Coil, a contemporary music group (and includes a track called 'How to Destroy an Angel'), but Jarman also includes parts of the Sea Interludes from Benjamin Britten's opera *Peter Grimes*.

Other attempts to film the Sonnets include Kevin Billington's series for Channel 4 in 1983. A sonnet would be read by a well-known actor in Elizabethan costume, for example Jane Lapotaire and Ben Kingsley, and then discussed by a prominent scholar or writer, for example A. L. Rowse and Gore Vidal (who interpreted Sonnet 35 as a reflection on buggery). A second and slightly different reading of the same sonnet then followed. Significant film interpretations of the Sonnets include Ang Lee's 1995 film version of Jane Austen's *Sense and Sensibility* (screenplay by Emma Thompson). Captain Willoughby (Greg Wise) has a flirtatious and insubstantial 'marriage of true minds' with Marianne Dashwood (Kate Winslet) as they discover their mutual fondness for Sonnet 116. After Marianne has been deserted by Willoughby, the sonnet remains for her a poignant focus of regret.

Sonnets as Music

Although, as we have seen, Shakespeare frequently used sonnet form in his plays, he never does so for passages that are intended to be sung. When he is writing words to be set to music he differentiates them from the surrounding text in several ways. He uses shorter verse lines, varied metrical forms, mixed rhymes, and refrains. His songs are generally less dense in style than his spoken dialogue, using more words than are strictly necessary to convey the sense. The reverse is usually true of his sonnets, which tend to be packed with meaning and complex in style. This no doubt helps to explain why the Sonnets have been far less frequently set to music than have the songs in the plays. Whereas settings of many of the songs by, for example, Thomas Arne, Franz Schubert, Richard Strauss, Gerald Finzi, Roger Quilter, Michael Tippett, John Dankworth, and other composers are frequently to be heard, even a dedicated music lover would be hard pressed to name more than one or two settings of the Sonnets, few of which have been recorded. Nevertheless, over the centuries a number of composers have risen to the challenge, even if most of their efforts have failed to enter the repertoire. The invaluably informative *Shakespeare Music Catalogue* (Oxford, 5 vols., 1991) records, for example, over 120 settings of the popular Sonnet 18 ('Shall I compare thee...'); John Dankworth's lyrical jazz version is particularly sensitive to the meaning of the words, especially as distinctively sung by Cleo Laine. On the other hand a number of the Sonnets have attracted only one composer, the indefatigable Richard Simpson (1820–76), who published an *Introduction to the Philosophy of Shakespeare's Sonnets* in 1868. Simpson was a Roman Catholic priest, a Shakespeare scholar, and an amateur composer who set not only every sonnet, some of them more than once, but many of the other poems, both authentic and spurious, as well. A few of his songs were posthumously published, but most of them survive only in manuscript in the British Library, unseen and unsung.

The first known setting of any of the sonnets probably dates from close to Shakespeare's lifetime, possibly even within it, though the earliest version to survive is in a manuscript dated 1659. It is a much-altered version of Sonnet 116 ('Let me not to the marriage of true minds'), beginning 'Self-blinding error seizeth all those minds', and was composed by Henry Lawes, the English court musician who lived from 1596 to 1662; he wrote the music for Milton's masque *Comus*, and took part in its first performance, at Ludlow Castle in 1634.

Most settings, however, date from the nineteenth century or later, many of them in translation into a wide range of languages, and most of them are for solo voice and piano, a form well suited to the setting of complex words. Hubert Parry, for example, set two of the sonnets. Some composers, however, have ventured on instrumental accompaniments. Among the finest of the latter is Benjamin Britten's version of Sonnet 43, 'When most I wink, then do mine eyes best see', the climax of his song cycle *Nocturne*, which sets poems concerned with night. Whatever the merits of considering the Sonnets in the context of the collection as a whole, to listen to this deeply felt, passionate union of words and music in relation to the other songs in Britten's cycle is to gain in understanding of the profound explorations of the paradoxes of darkness and light in Shakespeare's great poem to love and to the beloved.

Understandably, the sonnets that mention music have been particularly popular with composers. Igor Stravinsky set Sonnet 8 ('Music to hear') for voice, flute, clarinet, and piano, later arranging the accompaniment for piano alone; the same sonnet is one of many to be set for voice and piano by the Italian-born Mario Castelnuovo-Tedesco (1895–1968). Sonnet 128, 'How oft, when thou, my music, music play'st', has been the most popular among composers of the 'Dark Lady' Sonnets. In general this group of poems, which includes some of the most stylistically convoluted poems in the collection, has attracted relatively few composers—thirteen of the twenty-seven exist in three or fewer settings.[5] Sonnet 146—'Poor soul'—has even been adapted as a hymn (by Martin Shaw, collaborating with Ralph Vaughan Williams) included in the anthology *Songs of Praise*, and also by William Lowes Rushton in *The Shakespeare Hymn Tune Book* (1891).

One of the least typical, and least verbally complex, of the sonnets, Sonnet 66—'Tired with all these, for restful death I cry'—though it has not generally been highly regarded as poetry, has nevertheless been, during much of the twentieth century, one of the most genuinely popular as a song. In a fascinating essay Manfred Pfister identifies innumerable instances of its appropriation, especially though not only in musical settings, for political purposes in Eastern Europe and elsewhere, where the words 'art made tongue-tied by authority' (l. 9) have acquired special significance. It has become, Pfister writes, 'a commentary upon, an indictment of, the present times and the present world, the here and now, in which lovers find it hard to love and artists hard to work'.[6] Its political implications have sometimes been stressed by omitting the last line ('Save that to die I leave my love alone') and by free translation giving it a topical slant. Other versions, however, have emphasized the couplet's shift from political to personal issues. The great Russian composer Dimitri Shostakovitch composed three different versions of Sonnet 66 in a translation by Boris Pasternak, and it has also formed the basis for protest songs performed by popular singers. Among these is the German poet and songwriter Wolf Biermann, whose version, writes Pfister, 'cries out his and the sonnet's exasperation with great emotional intensity, modulating his voice from pathos to sarcasm and reinforcing his disgust at the seemingly endless catalogue of abuses with his own guitar accompaniment'.[7]

Affinities between the Sonnets and the plays are evident in the English composer Gustav Holst's use of two of them in his one-act opera *At the Boar's Head* (1924). This work, lasting under an hour and based largely on old English melodies, amalgamates passages centring on Falstaff from the scene in *1 Henry IV* in which Prince Hal challenges Falstaff's account of his exploits at Gadshill (2.5.114–486) with extracts from *2 Henry IV*, 2.5. Into these Holst incorporates two of Shakespeare's sonnets concerned with Time which underline the pathos of Falstaff's situation. As the old man sits the raddled whore Doll Tearsheet on his knee with the words 'I am old, I am old', the Prince sings Sonnet 19, 'Devouring Time, blunt thou the lion's paws'. A light orchestral accompaniment throws all possible emphasis on the words. Of this passage Holst writes, 'as the words deal chiefly with the ravages of Time upon the human face, they annoy Falstaff, who interrupts with the old ballad "When Arthur first in court began"'.[8] In Shakespeare's play Falstaff sings only a few words of the ballad, but Holst gives him an eight-stanza version sung as a duet with Doll and counterpointed with the Prince's singing of another time-centred sonnet, Sonnet 12, 'When I do count the clock that tells the time'. The tenor's long lyrical lines in juxtaposition with the hollow jauntiness of the ballad create a truly Shakespearian sense of emotional complexity.

Holst's counterpointing of one set of words against another had been anticipated by Sir Henry Bishop in his score for the Covent Garden adaptation of *The Two Gentlemen of Verona* of 1821, in which, oddly, a soloist sings four lines from Sonnet 2 ('When forty winters...') while another sings four from Sonnet 97 ('How like a winter...'). Bishop used lines from other sonnets, too, in his lightweight but charming, sub-Mozartean musical adaptations of several of Shakespeare's comedies. Settings of sonnets have also been incorporated in less heavily adapted versions of the plays, such as the Stratford Memorial Theatre production of *The Winter's Tale* of 1895, which included a setting, published as 'Fair, kind and true', by George Henschel of Sonnet 105. The device of simultaneity recurs in John Dankworth's 'Duet of Sonnets' (1964), in which Sonnets 23 ('As an unperfect actor...') and 24 ('Mine eye hath played the painter...') are sung to the same music, first separately and then together.

Sonnets have served as inspiration even for purely instrumental works. Writing of his heavily scored Second Piano Concerto (1969), Hans Werner Henze remarks that 'The "fantasia" of the third movement, where every traditional concept of form is abandoned, consists of a meditation on Shakespeare's sonnet "The expense of spirit in a waste of shame"'. And a passing reference in a song from Cole Porter's musical *Anything Goes* (1934) pays tribute to the Sonnets' reputation as supreme poems of love: 'You're the top':

> You're the top!
> You're the Colosseum,
> You're the top!
> You're the Louvre Museum,
> You're a melody from a symphony by Strauss.
> You're a Brendel bonnet,
> A Shakespeare sonnet,
> You're Mickey Mouse.

Hyper-productive of new meanings, in wildly different contexts, the Sonnets, like the beloved of Cole Porter's song, continue to inspire an inexhaustible catalogue of praise and modification. So, as Shakespeare foresaw, his sonnets take their place among the abiding monuments of Western civilization.

Notes

CHAPTER 1.   THE EARLY PUBLICATION OF THE SONNETS

1. Meres, *The Shakspere Allusion-Book*, ed. J. Munro, 2 vols. (London: Oxford University Press, 1932), 46–8.
2. MacDonald P. Jackson, 'Punctuation and the Compositors of *Shakespeare's Sonnets, 1609*', *Library*, 5th ser. 30 (1975), 1–24.
3. Pooler (Arden edn. 1918); Malone; Vendler; conjectured by Burrow.

CHAPTER 2.   THE HISTORY AND EMERGENCE OF THE SONNET AS A LITERARY FORM

1. Andrew Worrall, 'Richard Barnfield: A New Biography', *Notes and Queries* (Sept. 1992), 170–1, corrects Klawitter on Barnfield's biography, showing that he died in 1620, not 1627, and that there is no evidence that he married and had a son as previously believed, but that he had been disinherited in favour of his younger brother.

CHAPTER 3.   THE SONNETS IN RELATION TO SHAKESPEARE'S LIFE

1. *Supplemental Apology for the Believers in the Shakespeare Papers* (London: Thomas Egerton, 1799), 55.
2. Letters to George and Tom Keats, 21–27 Dec. 1817, and to Richard Woodhouse, 27 Oct, 1818, in *Letters*, ed. F. Page, World's Classics (London: Oxford University Press, 1954), 53 and 173.

CHAPTER 4.   THE FORM OF SHAKESPEARE'S SONNETS

1. See MacDonald P. Jackson, 'Rhymes in Shakespeare's Sonnets: Evidence of Date of Composition', *Notes and Queries*, 244 (1999), 213–19; 'Vocabulary and Chronology: The Case of Shakespeare's Sonnets', *Review of English Studies*, 205 (2001), 59–75; 'Dating Shakespeare's Sonnets: Some Old Evidence Revisited', *Notes and Queries*, 247 (2002), 237–41; 'The Distribution of Pronouns in *Shakespeare's Sonnets*', *Aumla: Journal of the Australasian Universities Language and Literature Association*, 97 (2002), 22–38. See Burrow,

pp. 105–6. Burrow's summary attempts to show that the first sixty poems date from around 1595–6—at the very height of the sonnet vogue, and at the time Shakespeare was writing the most sonnet-laden plays. Sonnets 61–103, it is proposed, date from 1594 to 1595, Sonnets 104–26 are thought to have been composed between 1598 and 1604, and Sonnets 127–54 are said to be the first written, between 1591 and 1595: 'they contain no late rare words' (Burrow, p. 106).

CHAPTER 5. THE ARTISTRY OF SHAKESPEARE'S SONNETS

1. For a longer discussion of the sonnet form in relation to the golden mean see *101 Sonnets from Shakespeare to Heaney*, ed. Don Paterson (London: Faber and Faber, 1999), pp. xv–xviii.

CHAPTER 6. CONCERNS OF THE SONNETS

1. Plato, *The Symposium*, trans. Walter Hamilton (Harmondsworth: Penguin, 1983), 87.
2. Ibid. 70.
3. Bruce R. Smith, 'Studies in Sexuality', in Stanley Wells and Lena Cowen Orlin (eds.), *Shakespeare: An Oxford Guide* (Oxford: Oxford University Press, 2003), 431–50: at 434.
4. John Florio's translation, with an introduction by Thomas Secombe, 3 vols. (London: Grant Richards, 1908), i. 234.
5. *A History of Gay Literature* (New Haven and London: Yale University Press, 1999), 394.
6. Stephen Orgel, *Impersonations: The Performance of Gender in Shakespeare's England* (Cambridge: Cambridge University Press, 1996), 57.

CHAPTER 7. THE SONNETS AS THEATRE

1. 'Metatheatre as Metaphorics: Playing Figures in Shakespeare's Sonnets', in G. Douglas Atkins and David M. Bergeron (eds.), *Shakespeare and Decon-struction*, 2nd edn. (New York: Peter Lang, 1991), 95–127: at 98.
2. *The Tragedy of King Lear*, 1.1.71.

CHAPTER 8. THE PLACE OF 'A LOVER'S COMPLAINT'

1. Kenneth Muir, '"A Lover's Complaint": A Reconsideration', in E. A. Bloom (ed.), *Shakespeare 1564–1964* (Providence, RI: 1964), 154–166; M. P. Jackson, *Shakespeare's 'A Lover's Complaint': Its Date and Authenticity* (Auckland: University of Auckland Press, English Series 13, 1965).

2. Sasha Roberts, *Reading Shakespeare's Poems in Early Modern England* (London: Palgrave Macmillan, 2003), 167, 151.
3. *The Mutual Flame: On Shakespeare's Sonnets and 'The Phoenix and the Turtle'* (London: Methuen, 1955), 33.

CHAPTER 10. THE CRITICAL REPUTATION OF THE SONNETS

1. Paul Morgan, 'Our Will Shakespeare and Lope de Vega: An Unrecorded Contemporary Document', *Shakespeare Survey, 16* (1963), 118–20: at 118.
2. Letter to John Hamilton Reynolds, 22 November 1817, in Keats, *Letters*, ed. F. Page, World's Classics (London: Oxford University Press, 1954), 45.
3. Letter to George and Georgianna Keats, 14 February to 3 May 1819, ibid. 271.
4. Jonathan Bate, *Shakespeare and the English Poetic Imagination* (Oxford: Oxford University Press, 1992), 182.
5. Ibid. 85.
6. Samuel Butler, *Shakespeare's Sonnets Reconsidered* (London: Jonathan Cape, 1899), 159.
7. Inga-Stina Ewbank, 'Shakespearean Strindberg: Influence as Insemination', in J. Batchelor et al. (eds.), *Shakespearean Continuities* (London: Macmillan, 1997), 339.
8. *Shakespeare's Lives*, 2nd edn. (Oxford: Oxford University Press, 1991), 320.
9. Cited in H. Montgomery Hyde, *Oscar Wilde* (London: Methuen, 1976), 329.
10. Manchester and New York: Manchester University Press, 1997, 8.
11. Ibid. 236–8.
12. *Overruled, and The Dark Lady of the Sonnets* (London: Constable, 1927), 179.
13. Masefield, *William Shakespeare* (London: Williams and Norgate, 1911), 247.
14. San Marino, Calif.: Huntington Library, 1981, 155.
15. Logan Pearsall Smith, *On Reading Shakespeare* (London: Constable, 1933), 8–9.
16. Cited in James Schiffer (ed.), *Shakespeare's Sonnets: Critical Essays* (New York and London: Garland Publishing, 2000), 38–9.
17. Cited in Schiffer (ed.), *Shakespeare's Sonnets*, 36.
18. Cited in John Gross, *After Shakespeare* (Oxford: Oxford University Press, 2000), 25.

CHAPTER II.   THE SONNETS AND LATER WRITERS

1. Phillis Levin (ed.), *The Penguin Book of the Sonnet* (London: Penguin, 2001), 179.

2. *A History of Gay Literature: The Male Tradition* (New Haven and London: Yale University Press, 1998), 119.

3. In *Shakespeare and the Victorians* (London: Thomson Learning, 2004), ch. 5, Adrian Poole notices echoes of Sonnet 1 in lyric 38, l. 6; of Sonnet 43 in lyric 57, l. 5; of Sonnets 77 and 59 in lyric 117, ll. 9–12; and Sonnet 144 in lyric 102, ll. 7–8.

4. *Mrs Dalloway* (1992; repr. Harmondsworth: Penguin, 2000), 82.

5. *Nothing Like the Sun* (London: William Heinemann Ltd, 1964; repr. Vintage, 1992), 11.

6. Cited in Jan Morris, *Venice* (1960; 3rd rev. edn., London: Faber and Faber, 1993), 300.

7. Erica Jong, *Serenissima* (1986; repr. London: Bloomsbury, 1997), 4–5. Further page references appear in the text.

8. Lennard J. Davis, *The Sonnets: A Novel* (Albany, NY: State University of New York Press, 2001), 9 and 63.

9. Ibid. 11.

10. Mark Lamos, Introduction to *Love's Fire* by Eric Bogosian, William Finn, John Guare, Tony Kushner, Marsha Norman, Ntozake Shange, Wendy Wasserstein (New York: William Morrow, 1998), p. xii. Further page references appear in the text.

11. *Shakespeare's R & J* (London: Methuen, 2003 edn), 2.

12. The numbering is Helen Gardner's; *John Donne: The Divine Poems*, ed. Helen Gardner (Oxford: Oxford University Press, 1952).

13. Margaret Edson, *Wit* (New York: Faber and Faber, 1999), 14–15.

CHAPTER 12.   THE SONNETS IN PERFORMANCE

1. Edith Evans reads her own selection of twenty sonnets arranged into four bands on an apparently undated Columbia Long Playing Record: Nos. 91, 18, 15, 2, 8; 52, 27, 61, 73, 66; 33, 57, 97, 56, 104; 106, 23, 116, 94, 29.

2. George Rylands, *The Sonnets*, leaflet accompanying the recording (London: Argo, 1958).

3. Simon Callow, *Being an Actor* (London: Methuen, 1984), 102, 104–5. Callow explains John Padel's reordering of the Sonnets in detail on pp. 100–3.

4. Peter J. Smith, '*Sweet Sessions*', in *Cahiers Élisabéthains*, 40 (Oct. 1991), 84–6.

5. They are Nos. 127, 131, 132, 134, 135, 136, 141, 142, 143, 145, 150, 151, and 152; the last two of these have been set only by Richard Simpson.

6. 'Route 66: The Political Performance of Shakespeare's Sonnet 66 in Germany and Elsewhere', in A. Luis Pujante and Ton Hoenselaars (eds.), *Four Hundred Years of Shakespeare in Europe* (New York and London: University of Delaware Press, 2003), 70–88: at 81.

7. Ibid.

8. Cited in the booklet accompanying the recording conducted by David Atherton, EMI Records Ltd., CDM 5651272

Further Reading

This section aims to provide suggestions for reading that will extend and deepen understanding of the topics discussed in this book. It is not intended as a list of all the books mentioned in the text, or consulted in writing it. A helpful survey of criticism is included in the anthology listed under Schiffer below. Ongoing criticism and scholarship are reviewed in the annual *Shakespeare Survey*, published by Cambridge University Press. Editions of the Sonnets are surveyed in Chapter 9.

Barnfield, Richard, *The Complete Poems*, ed. George Klawitter (Selinsgrove: Susquehanna University Press, 1990): a scholarly edition with excellent editorial material.

Booth, Stephen, *An Essay on Shakespeare's Sonnets* (New Haven: Yale University Press, 1969): a modestly entitled, enduringly useful book which suggests a variety of close readings.

Briggs, A. D. P (ed.), *English Sonnets* (London: Dent, 1999): a useful anthology, which contains several of the sonnets by writers other than Shakespeare referred to in Chapter 11.

Burgess, Anthony, *Nothing Like the Sun* (London: William Heinemann, 1964; repr. Vintage, 1992): a vibrant and witty novel which refers to the Sonnets throughout in relation to Shakespeare's life.

Davis, Lennard J., *The Sonnets: A Novel* (Albany, NY: State University of New York Press, 2001): a reimagining of situations suggested by the Sonnets as a novel of academic life.

Empson, William, *Seven Types of Ambiguity* (London: Chatto and Windus, 1930): a seminal work of close criticism which includes remarks on the Sonnets.

—— *Some Versions of Pastoral* (London: Chatto and Windus, 1935): includes an essay on Sonnet 94.

Evans, Maurice (ed.), *Elizabethan Sonnets* (London: Dent, 1977): an anthology of sonnet sequences and selected sonnets by Sidney, Daniel, Drayton, Spenser, Lodge, and other contemporaries of Shakespeare.

Fineman, Joel, *Shakespeare's Perjured Eye: The Invention of Poetic Subjectivity in the Sonnets* (Berkeley and Los Angeles: University of California Press, 1986): a dense and theorized study of the poetic persona of the Sonnets, its radical position in literary tradition, the early modern period, and subsequent understandings of literary subjectivity.

Fenton, James, 'Auden on Shakespeare's Sonnets', in *The Strength of Poetry* (Oxford: Oxford University Press, 2001): a subtle recontextualization of W. H. Auden's Signet introduction to the Sonnets, and one which engages with other discussions of sexuality.

Fuller, John (ed.), *The Oxford Book of Sonnets* (Oxford: Oxford University Press, 2000): a useful anthology, which contains several of the sonnets by writers other than Shakespeare referred to in Chapter 11.

Fumerton, Patricia, *Cultural Aesthetics: Renaissance Literature and the Practice of Social Ornament* (Chicago: University of Chicago Press, 1991): a discussion of the Renaissance practice of portrait miniatures and sonneteering as closely related activities, crucial to the development of subjective awareness.

Gurr, Andrew, 'Shakespeare's First Poem: Sonnet 145', *Essays in Criticism*, 21 (1971), 221–6.

Hammond, Paul, *Figuring Sex between Men from Shakespeare to Rochester* (Clarendon Press: Oxford University Press, 2002): an excellent discussion of seventeenth-century literary presentations of sex between men, with a section on the Sonnets.

Hilský, Martin, '"Telling what is told": Original, Translation and the Third Text—Shakespeare's Sonnets in Czech', in A. Luis Pujante and Ton Hoenselaars (eds.), *Four Hundred Years of Shakespeare in Europe* (Newark and London: University of Delaware Press, 2003), 134–44.

Jakobson, Roman (with L. G. Jones), 'Shakespeare's Verbal Art in "Th' Expence of Spirit"', in Roman Jakobson, *Language in Literature*, ed. Krystyna Pomorska and Stephen Rudy (Boston: Harvard University Press, 1987), 198–215: a brilliantly detailed study of the grammatical construction of Sonnet 129.

Jones, Peter (ed.), *The Sonnets: A Casebook* (London: Macmillan, 1977): includes much of the best comment and criticism up to 1976.

Jong, Erica, *Serenissima* (1986; repr. London: Bloomsbury, 1997): a sexy and amusing novel which uses the Sonnets as the premiss for a biographical adventure.

Knight, G. Wilson, *The Mutual Flame: On Shakespeare's Sonnets and 'The Phoenix and the Turtle'* (London: Methuen, 1955): an idiosyncratic study by a major critic.

Leishman, James B., *Themes and Variations in Shakespeare's Sonnets* (London: Hutchinson, 1961): a useful exploration of the Sonnets' relationship to classical literature.

Lever, J. W., *The Elizabethan Love Sonnet* (London: Methuen, 1974): a valuable critical survey.

Levin, Phillis (ed.), *The Penguin Book of the Sonnet: 500 Years of a Classic Tradition in English* (London: Penguin Books, 2001): a useful anthology, which contains several of the sonnets by writers other than Shakespeare referred to in Chapter 11.

Magnusson, Lynne, 'Non-Dramatic Poetry', in Stanley Wells and Lena Orlin (eds.), *Shakespeare: An Oxford Guide* (Oxford: Oxford University Press, 2003), 286–307.

Melchiori, Giorgio, *Shakespeare's Dramatic Meditations: An Experiment in Criticism* (Oxford: Oxford University Press, 1976), a highly detailed close and contextualized study of Sonnets 94, 121, 129, and 146.

Muir, Kenneth, *Shakespeare's Sonnets* (London: Allen and Unwin, 1979): a useful handbook of commentary and a guide to some of the major areas of sonnet criticism.

Paterson, Don (ed.), *101 Sonnets from Shakespeare to Heaney* (London: Faber and Faber, 1999): a useful anthology, which contains several of the sonnets by writers other than Shakespeare referred to in Chapter 11.

Pequigney, Joseph, *Such is My Love: A Study of Shakespeare's Sonnets* (Chicago and London: University of Chicago Press, 1985): a strongly and intelligently homoerotic reading of the Sonnets.

Pfister, Manfred, 'Route 66: The Political Performance of Shakespeare's Sonnet 66 in Germany and Elsewhere', in A. Luis Pujante and Ton Hoenselaars (eds.), *Four Hundred Years of Shakespeare in Europe* (Newark and London: University of Delaware Press, 2003), 70–88.

Schalkwyk, David, *Speech and Performance in Shakespeare's Sonnets and Plays* (Cambridge: Cambridge University Press, 2002): a philosophically engaged study of the performative quality of language in the Sonnets in relation to the plays.

Schiffer, James (ed.), *Shakespeare's Sonnets: Critical Essays* (New York and London: Garland Publishing, 2000): an excellent collection of new and reprinted essays preceded by the editor's valuable long introduction 'Reading New Life into Shakespeare's Sonnets: A Survey of Criticism'. Schiffer provides a survey of all the major critical approaches as represented in monographs, articles, and collections of essays.

Smith, Bruce R., *Homosexual Desire in Shakespeare's England: A Cultural Poetics* (Chicago: Chicago University Press, 1991): includes discussion of sonnets addressed to a male in relation to the history of love between men in Renaissance England.

Smith, Hallett, '"No Cloudy Stuffe to Puzzle Intellect": A Testimonial Misapplied to Shakespeare', *Shakespeare Quarterly*, 1 (1950), 18–21: a neglected brief article demonstrating Benson's plagiarism in his preface.

Spiller, Michael G., *The Development of the Sonnet* (London: Routledge, 1992): a study of the development of the sonnet form from its beginnings to Milton.

Warren, Roger, 'Why Does it End Well? Helena, Bertram and the Sonnets', *Shakespeare Survey*, 22 (Cambridge, 1969), 79–92: an exploration of narratives in the Sonnets in relation to *All's Well That Ends Well*.

Wells, Stanley, *Looking for Sex in Shakespeare* (Cambridge: Cambridge University Press, 2004): includes a chapter on the originality of the Sonnets.

Wilde, Oscar, *The Portrait of Mr W. H.*, is available in many reprints of both the original, shorter version (in e.g. *Complete Short Fiction*, ed. Ian Small, Harmondsworth: Penguin Books, 1995) and the revision first published complete in 1921; references to the latter are to the 1958 reprint edited by Vyvyan Holland and published by Methuen.

On the internet, *The Amazing Website of Shakespeare's Sonnets* http://www.shakespeares-sonnets.com/ provides access to a wide range of texts including a facsimile of the 1609 Quarto, annotated texts of the Sonnets, and texts of sequences by Thomas Wyatt and by Shakespeare's contemporaries. Other websites come and go, but may be traced through use of a search engine.